Never Give Up On A Dream

A Guide for Living Your Dreams

Never Give Up On A Dream
© 2023 by Loria Raiola-Trapp, M.Ed.

Published by: Soul Power International, LLC

All rights reserved. No part of this book may be used or reproduced in any manner whatsoever, nor may it be stored in a retrieval system, transmitted, or otherwise copied for public or private use, without written permission, except in the case of brief quotations embodied in critical articles or reviews.

Book Cover Design: Terry Z
Editor: Pam Murphy

Paperback ISBN: 979-8-9886091-0-0
eBook ISBN: 979-8-9886091-1-7

Printed in the United States of America

Never Give Up On A Dream

A Guide for Living Your Dreams

Loria Raiola-Trapp, M.Ed.

Testimonials

"Ever considered abandoning a long-held dream? Put the brakes on that idea as you let Loria's 12-year fertility journey guide your way. She will take you on a roller coaster of emotions from laughter to tears as you read how persistence in heart and soul fuels fulfillment. Sprinkled throughout the book are practical wisdoms, resources and support personalized for your unique success. A must read!"
~ Tianna Conte, N.D., Best-selling author of *Love's Fire Series: Beyond Mortal Boundaries* and *Living the Awakened Journey*

"Whether you are a beginner or advanced seeker on the road to living your dreams, there will be something in this book that you can use and apply to keep you flowing towards your heart's desire."
~ Robin George, Owner of Wink Photography

"Waiting for a dream to manifest can be a long and arduous journey. In *Never Give Up On A Dream*, Loria provides a guide that will get you through."
~ Miriam Pratt, CEO and part owner at Superior Clinical Care

"Loria's journey has given me the inspiration, drive and motivation to stick with my dream even when things do not go my way. 'She did it and so can I.'"
~ Min Guo, Master of International Studies, Washington University

"Loria provides a guide that leads to self-empowerment. She shows us how to align with what it is that wants to create by going with the flow as we wait on the Will of Heaven."

~ Steve Daurio, Ph.D, Counseling Psychologist

"Never Give Up On A Dream encourages every person to love, respect, honor and cherish themselves with the awareness that we are all spiritual beings having a very, very, very human experience. Imagine if we all had that awareness? The world as we know it would cease to exist!"

~ Rosita Roldan, dancer/choreographer and visual artist

Dedication

Dream, dream, dream, dream, dream, dream, dream, dream, dream dream…. dream it in technicolor, dream it in play, dream it by evening, dream it by day!!

What do you desire? What do you see? When the impossible is possible, it's meant for me! What is your vision? What is at stake? What are you giving? What will you take?

What dreams return, though you might put them down? They won't go away. They come back around!

What are you drawn to? What intrigues or inspires? Rising higher and higher to your heart's desire.

Are angels or doubters chewing your ear? Can you separate love from fear?

Who said you can't have it? We know you can!

Don't wish, make it happen and follow a plan!

What is yours will come to you. Going with flow is what you must do!

When the dream you envision lives in your heart, you know that you're ready to make a new start.

Your decision is made, now you enact. Take one step towards your dream, it will take one hundred steps back!

Remember to laugh, remember to play, take care of yourself, that's the best way.

So, dream in the morning. Dream in the night. Dreamer's dream, dreams held in their sight.

I honor and support your dedication towards living the dream of your heart's desire whatever that may be. Any passion we are drawn to is worth the dream and the time it takes to get there.

Outrageous blessings, ease and grace on the road to living your wildest dreams.

~ **Loria Ra**

Acknowledgments

Never Give Up On A Dream would not be complete without acknowledging the many people who have inspired, supported, loved and encouraged me during my life journey. There is not enough room here to formally thank all who have embraced me or taught me something new about myself. I remain blessed by knowing you! For now, I'd like to express my gratitude to the following individuals who stand out in my heart. My life has been enriched because of you!

Pam Murphy, my publisher and editor at *My Book, My Passion Publishing* and her team, for being so accommodating, patient, and making the birth of my first book so easy. I value your expertise and input. I trust your wisdom. Thank you for reaching out to me during the regrouping process when I needed to get the ball rolling again! Wishing you every success moving forward.

The late Viki Winterton, founder of *Experts Insights Publishing*. Thank you for your wisdom, expertise, vision, support and enthusiasm for writers. I am very happy that people like you exist in our world!

Dr. Tianna Conte (Tianna), Best-Selling Author of *Love's Fires Trilogies* and founder of GPS-Code™, for giving me the title of this book, *Never Give Up On A Dream*, which resonated deep into my soul, and for your very special mentorship, love, vision, inspiration and support throughout the decades. What a ride it has been! Being in the world but not of it has been a blast!! A billion blessings *your* way!!!

Thunderous thanks to my logo designer Laurie Bain. You are an exceptional visionary artist and primal painter. Thank you for your beautiful and moving artwork.

The late Blanca Beyar, *shaman, spiritual teacher and author*, whose seventeen books inspired me to get going on my first of more to come.

The late Sajda Musawwir Ladner, Artistic and Creative Director of Universal Temple of The Arts, for her inspiration, friendship, creative collaboration, mentorship and vision. We had so much fun creating together and hanging out! I miss you! (But I know you're just fine where you are stylin'!!)

Christine Raiola, my mother, for being my first spiritual teacher, your unconditional love and strength have been a source of stability for me in this life and beyond. Thank you for holding up the office of *Grandmother*. It means so much to all of us. You are an amazing Nona to Daniel and Jermain. Seriously Mom, you make the world's best red sauce! I'm blessed to have chosen you as my mother!

The late Joseph Raiola, my father, Grandpa Joe, for valuing and exposing me to alternative medicine, holistic health care and yoga at a young age. You always encouraged me to seek the truth by doing my own research, questioning narratives and becoming educated. That served me well on my journey, Dad. We do keep your memory alive! Eternal love and admiration.

Joe Raiola and Bill Raiola, my brothers, who by their dedication to our mother have allowed me to relocate knowing that she is well taken care of and safe in her own home. Mom is blessed to have such committed sons as you. What great guys you are! May your kindness come back to you one thousandfold!

Jermain and Daniel Trapp, our twin sons, now fifteen years of age, are constantly teaching me the meaning of love, patience, understanding and parenting in a greater way than I had previously known. You have both taught me so much! Remember we're in this world together! Love you both to the stars and back!

Karlus Trapp, my best friend, husband, *Baby Daddy,* music man, collaborator, and *joy bringer,* thank you for holding up the fort when I went to write late nights at the Gulf Gate Library. Thank you for teaching our boys what it means to be a man by your living example. So priceless! Your unconditional love, support, dedication, inspiration and sense of humor all these years has made me a very blessed woman!

Women of the GPS-Code™ Inner Circle: Tianna Conte, Carole Dubs, Denice Galicia, Jessa Grace and the late Mary Azima Jackson. Each one of you has empowered me in your own way. Thank you for holding space for me through these potent, powerful and unprecedented times, each with your own unique gifts, perspectives, support and voice. I love flying with the eagles and do not intend to ever come down! May the wind always be at your back!

To my high vibrational besties in this world who have stood by my side through thick and thin! Your love and support have been immeasurable and priceless! I admire you for the high frequency you hold and the creative gifts you share with the world. Love you always, Nubia Braithwaite for your fierce strength, Rosita Roldan for your fierce passion, Doreen Overstrom for your loving heart, Linda Hall for your dedication, Denise Becker for your wisdom, Robin George for your truth, Ellen Looft for your kindness, Jeannine Otis for the joy you bring, Erica Zuber for your example and Colleen Kubinski for your friendship.

Willie Chu and Robin George, Wink Photography, for your friendship, artistic and creative support on many of my projects all these years.

Joan Caddell, Divine Women, LLC, for your courage, inspiration and beauty.

Jessa Grace for your creative and technical support.

Coach Carmen Abercrombie of *Sharing the Bliss* for your creative and business support, which served to expand my knowledge on the road to serving others.

Anthony Abercrombie for your videographic, creative and technical support and collaboration on *The Five Tibetan Rites, Journey to Empowerment.*

David Schmidt, CEO and Founder of Lifewave, for having a genius miracle mind and directing it towards the upliftment of humanity. I am so very grateful to ride this wave that you have created.

For the following master teachers who I have had the privilege of training with: Derek O'Neil, *SQ Wellness*, the late Elizabeth Mass, teacher of *The Course in Miracles* and Stevan Thayer, Founder of *Integrated Energy Therapy,* for showing me and giving me the skills to heal so that I may live my best life and share my gifts. The work was deep, intense at times but oh so joyful. I bow to you!

The late Maya Angelou for your inspiration through your recordings, writings and your model of excellence and honesty in the literary arts.

And finally, for my Higher Power, Good God Almighty for always being there with eternal love, support, grace, direction, protection and guidance. Thank you. Thank you. Thank you.

Table of Contents

Introduction 15

PART ONE — DREAM ESSENTIALS
Chapter 1   My Body Is the Temple of The Divine, or Is It? 19
Chapter 2   Our Auric Field 21
Chapter 3   Our Physical Body 25
Chapter 4   Our Emotional Body 29
Chapter 5   Our Mental Body 35
Chapter 6   Our Spiritual Body 43
Chapter 7   Listening to Your Intuition 49
Chapter 8   The Universal Law of Vibration 55
Chapter 9   The Law of Attraction 59
Chapter 10 Affirmations 65
Chapter 11 The Power of Forgiveness 69
Chapter 12 The Love Vibration 75
Chapter 13 The Fear Vibration 79

PART TWO — HOW BIG CAN YOU DREAM
Chapter 14 Dream Journey 87
Chapter 15 Against All Odds 91
Chapter 16 Find Out What You Are Made Of! 95
Chapter 17 What Is Yours Will Come to You 97
Chapter 18 Guard and Protect Your Precious Energy 101
Chapter 19 Open to Possibilities Is the Way to Go! 103
Chapter 20 Soul Speak 107
Chapter 21 Act As If, Until the Real Thing Comes Along 111

Chapter 22	Stoking the Fires of Desire	115
Chapter 23	When a Dream Dies	119
Chapter 24	Dream Tripping	121
Chapter 25	Holding Vision	123
Conclusion		125
An Invitation to Be Part of Our Community		127
About the Author		131

Introduction

Living Your Dreams

*"Be fearless in the pursuit of what
sets your soul on fire."*
~ Jennifer Lee

Namaste and Good Day!

My name is Loria Raiola-Trapp (AKA Angel Yogi Loria Ra) and I believe that people are most fulfilled and happy when they are living their dreams. For the very things that you are drawn to repeatedly, those very experiences that light you up like a Christmas tree, those very things that make your heart sing and dance with delight and joy are the very things that you were meant to live and share.

If you're anything like me, and I would bet you are or you would not have picked up this book, you just might envision yourself as I do: A woman who swims with the dolphins, dances with the gypsies, flies with the eagles and rubs ripe mangos all over her body! (Well, maybe only the last one occasionally!)

What about you? How do you envision yourself? What is one thing about yourself that you can truly embrace? What makes you truly unique?

Please do not underestimate the importance of play, laughter and self-care on the road to living your dreams, traveling the path towards enlightenment. We have all experienced living some of our dreams and observed how other dreams have manifested quickly. Often dreams have taken years or decades to be fulfilled. Some dreams we are still yearning for and others we will take to our graves; perhaps living them in our next incarnation.

Hold on to them and keep them close to your heart as our dreams never have to stop because we are *eternal beings*. Quantum physics teaches us that energy cannot be created or destroyed. Changed yes. Destroyed no!

Never Give Up on A Dream!

Or, as Nelson Mandela asserts, *"A winner is a dreamer who never gives up!"*

How to Use This Book

This book was written as a guide to living a more expanded life as you live your dreams. The tools, exercises and techniques herein were designed to take you into a deeper knowing, understanding and respect of your *divine gifts* endowed to you from *The Creator*. In this book, *The Creator* is interchangeable with the words: *God, God Source, Divine Mother, Divine Father, Universe, Ascended Masters, Beings of Light, Angelic Host, Supreme Love,* or fill in whomever sources your higher power.

Each chapter in this book is complete unto itself. You can read and complete the exercises in the order in which it was written or skip around. Part I of the book offers a nuts-and-bolts awareness reminder as to how we operate as spiritual humans. In Part II, I share more about how I apply practical and spiritual techniques for navigation and success on my journey.

Be sure to see *The Invitation To Be Part of Our Community* so that we can continue to be a resource for Soul Power Support during good times, challenging times and everything in between.

Ready to dream on? Here we go!!!

PART ONE

Dream Essentials

"When you wish upon a star
makes no difference who you are
anything your heart desires will come to you."

~ Ned Washington

CHAPTER 1

My Body Is the Temple of The Divine—or Is It?

"Treat yourself like a precious gift because that will keep you strong." ~ *Julia Cameron*

I love that quote and would only add to it: Treat yourself like a precious *divine* gift because that is who you truly are!

Have you heard the phrase by Pierre Teilhard de Chardin, *"We are spiritual beings having a human experience?"* What does it mean to you? If you believe that you were created in the image of your *God-Source,* then you are **more** than just a mere mortal but not **less** than a human being. When we embrace both our *humanness* **and** our *spiritual divine nature,* we are living a life connected to our higher power, divine guidance and *soul path* on earth. This makes our journey a lot easier!

So, what is self-care and why is it so important?

Self-care can be defined as the daily practices and routines that support your life force and nurture your body and *Soul.* On the road to living your dreams, you will want to keep your body in tip-top shape. What does that have to do with living our dreams, you ask?

Everything!

Like a well-tuned automobile, cruising through life beats losing time, energy and momentum any day and that's no fun!

Self-care supports you in living your life's purpose in a greater way. It allows you to show up for yourself first and then others. The good news is that The Creator has endowed us with *free will,* so we get to choose *how* we are going to travel, what we are going to put into our bodies and minds and how we are going to care for our precious vehicle. We get to decide how we are going to direct our precious energy. Think about it. Would you prefer to travel through time in a rusted Ford pickup, roller skates or a Rolls Royce, Corvette, Tesla or something else?

We have the option of traveling through time kicking and screaming or we can *go with the flow.* As spiritual beings having a very human experience, kicking and screaming most certainly has its place but *living there* is going to cost us our health.

Our bodies are the vessels that we travel through time in. One day we will drop them and move on. Where we are going, I am not sure, but I do know that your essence will never die nor will mine.

The Law of Conservation of Energy states that energy can neither be created nor destroyed, only transformed so that it can be used. This means that energy is never lost, only transformed from one form to another. For example, solar panels do not create solar energy. They harness energy from the sun and transform it into another type of energy (electricity). In truth, there is no death! We are eternal beings.[1]

---

[1] At this time in our evolution, there are thousands of testimonials recorded in the literature of individuals who have experienced NDEs (near death experiences), whose stories collaborate on being reunited with loved ones, going through a tunnel of white light and who receive a non-judgmental life review in the presence of astonishing love. These individuals return from their NDEs transformed, with profound information to live and share, as well as deeper understandings and greater gifts to navigate this world. These events would be foolish to discount.

CHAPTER 2

Our Auric Field

"The whole is more than the sum of its parts." ~ *Aristotle*

From an energetic point of view, our auric field can be visualized as oval layers of energy that reflect and hold imprints of our past and present physical health, life experiences, belief systems, emotions, dreams and aspirations. In other words, the auric field reflects the state of being and overall health of an individual. Each hidden layer has a color, meaning, and purpose. Some people can see auras, and everyone can feel them. One way to think about auras is as the energy you feel emitting from a person or animal around you.

In this book, we will be dealing with the first four layers of the auric field. They are the physical, emotional, mental, and spiritual bodies (layers). These four bodies continually interact, communicate, and dynamically inform each other from the moment we are born until the day we pass.

As an example, being cyberbullied is emotional abuse, which affects the emotional body of the individual being abused. Most of the time, emotional abuse affects a person's self-esteem (mental body) negatively, especially if it is ongoing. Ongoing emotional abuse often leads to physical symptoms such as stomachaches, sleep disturbances, ulcers, etc., or they may come to feel so bad about themselves that they do not believe they are good enough to deserve happiness. This belief cuts them off from their divinity and can lead to suicidal ideations or actual suicide.

When we nurture one or more of our bodies, it supports the other bodies. As an example, the simple act of giving yourself a hug (physical body) can release the feel-good hormone called oxytocin in your body. That's why hugs are so powerful in bonding. So can cuddling, giving someone a massage or making love. This in turn regulates our emotional responses (emotional body) and pro-social behaviors including positive communication, empathy, bonding, trust and lifts our mood.

Similarly, when we go hiking in nature, our muscles and bones strengthen as our physical body releases endorphins, which lift our emotional mood. Good sleep affects our mood and mental focus. If we *think* positively (mental body), it affects how we *feel* (emotional body) during the day.

Time For Reflection

Can you recall a time when your positive attitude, laughter, or light heartedness affected those around you? In what way? Explain.

_____
_____
_____
_____
_____
_____
_____
_____

Our Auric Field

_____
_____

It works in reverse too. Can you recall a time when you were emotionally upset and lost your cool or reacted in a way that was not for your highest good? How did that affect you? What about those you interacted with?

_____
_____
_____
_____
_____
_____
_____
_____
_____

• • •

This book will encourage you to express your angry feelings in a healthy way and not stuff your emotions inside. We've all stuffed our feelings at one time or another as a survival skill or to please others at our own expense. The good news is that we have real solutions. When those sad, angry, shameful, rageful, guilty and fearful emotions emerge, they are ready to be released; *not* on to someone, but expressed in a safe, private space. The more healed we are, the freer we are to live our dreams through joy.

CHAPTER 3

Our Physical Body

"Your body is a Temple." ~ *Corinthians 6:19-20*

The more modern quote, "*My Body is The Temple of The Divine*" is not just a new age cliché as its wisdom goes back to the Upanishads,[2] written about 1500-1200 BCE.

Our **physical body** is the vessel that contains our physical form and our spiritual container. It is the storing house of our emotions and thoughts. It performs many functions that support us in maintaining the conditions necessary for life, for example: breathing and blood circulation, and allows us to accomplish those things which are important to us. Caring for our physical body includes the quality of the food, air, nourishment and water we take in.

Our physical body speaks to us all the time through sensations of pleasure and pain.

---

2   The *Upanishads* are documents that contain the central teachings of Hinduism. *Upanishad* means to sit with or sit next to the enlightened ones. The main idea of the *Upanishads* is that Brahman, the supreme force of the universe, is permanently connected to humanity. By following their responsibility in life, individuals can break the cycle of death and rebirth and become unified with Brahman. No definite date can be ascribed to the composition of the Vedas of which The *Upanishads* is part of, but the period of about 1500-1200 BCE is acceptable to most scholars.

Time For Reflection

Do you agree that your body is the Temple of The Divine? If so, how does that support you in taking care of it?

_____
_____
_____
_____
_____
_____
_____

How is your diet? Are you drinking enough clean water? Are you getting adequate rest to renew? How do you keep it clean? How do you keep it safe?

_____
_____
_____
_____
_____
_____
_____
_____
_____
_____

What daily or weekly practices and rituals do you have that support, love, and nourish your physical vessel? Practices can include

Our Physical Body

using a Waterpik daily, practicing yoga, walking, basketball, meditation, getting massages, using light patch technology, working with a healthcare professional, utilizing a specific vitamin protocol, etc.

_____
_____
_____
_____
_____
_____
_____
_____
_____

Are there any excesses? What habits or addictions do you have that take energy away from your body? Example: drinking an excess of caffeine, sodas or energy drinks, smoking cigarettes, vaping, emotional eating, etc.

_____
_____
_____
_____
_____
_____
_____
_____
_____

<u>Never Give Up On a Dream</u>

What is one habit you can put in place right now to further support your body? Example: drinking more water or going to bed 15 minutes earlier on a work night.

_____
_____
_____
_____
_____
_____
_____

• • •

Give yourself a mental pat on the back for taking this inventory. Looking at your current self-care in the now will best support you moving forward on the road towards living your dreams.

Remember the more love you show your physical body, the more love your body will show you. You as a **shining star** are so worth it!

CHAPTER 4

Our Emotional Body

"I can show you the world, shining, shimmering, splendid.
Tell me Princess, now when did you last
Let your heart decide?" ~ *Tim Rice*

    Our **emotional body** encompasses the feelings that we have towards ourselves, family, friends, significant others, our work and the relationship to the world around us. Our *emotional body* oversees how we give and receive love. A healthy emotional body can give and receive love in balance, express emotions, and be able to sustain positive significant relationships and relationships with co-workers.
    Our *emotional body* embraces the full array of our human emotions including guilt, betrayal, shame, joy, love, judgment, jealousy, anger, resentment, rage, stress, fear and everything in between. Having feelings and complex emotions are part of what makes us human. This is a gift which makes us stand out as a species.
    Our emotional body speaks to us all the time through our feelings.
    Our *emotional body* functions like a divine messaging system in that it will **inform you through your feelings**. Your feelings will deliver a message to guide you in the direction of your **soul's path**. All you must do is listen. In this way, you can allow emotions to be your guide. They are meant to be listened to, felt, expressed and released.

E-motions are truly energy in motion!
When viewed this way, emotions are truly a God-given navigation system that can take you closer to understanding your life's purpose and living your dreams.

Our emotions are felt through the portal of our heart. Did you know that the heart holds a higher frequency than even the brain? Yes, your heart is the most powerful source of electromagnetic energy in your body. It produces the largest rhythmic electromagnetic field of any of the body's organs. The heart's electrical field is about sixty times greater in amplitude than the electrical activity generated by the brain!

This book encourages you to express your emotions and not stuff them. What does that have to do with living your dreams you might wonder?

The short answer is that emotions stored in the body take up space. They clutter the energy body and prevent us from living our lives fully. If not expressed, they often fester resulting in states of dis-ease.

Cellular memory encompasses the memories, traumas and unresolved feelings that the emotional body will store in the cells of our bodies until these emotions are ready to be released and healed. Our body can store emotions for years, decades and lifetimes. The *emotional body* can release these feelings through the physical body as part of its healing process.

• • •

Cora's story: A woman, who we shall call Cora, stuffed her feelings of anger into her body for decades. She became so obsessed with her resentment towards her sister-in-law that she could not enjoy the holidays with her own family. She wound up hating the holidays and robbed herself and her family of the joy that they could bring.

Instead of working through her smoldering feelings of deep anger, she preferred to hang on to them. She wore this anger like a banner of justified righteous indignation, which only grew bigger and bigger over time. This anger took up an immense amount of Cora's thought processes, creative energy and constructive time resulting in depression, self-loathing, guilt and self-pity.

Finally, Cora sought help and worked with a spiritual therapist who supported her in expressing and releasing her resentment towards her sister-in-law. Eventually she was able to forgive starting with herself first. In time, she forgave her sister-in-law. The key was her openness to starting the healing process.

Today Cora can enjoy the holidays with her family in a much greater way. She is no longer a prisoner of her emotions and no longer *attached* to her feelings about what her sister-in-law did or did not do. To Cora, it now feels like what had transpired was no big deal. Although to this day, she does not keep in touch with her sister-in-law, she is at peace knowing that true forgiveness is something we do for ourselves first to set ourselves free from the incident or event.

• • •

Acknowledging and feeling our emotions so that we can heal is the first step to clearing our emotional body. Remember, expressing emotions is very healthy, even though that is something that many cultures do not encourage. Raging on another is not the way to go about expressing your feelings because that could not only make it worse for you but it could even put you in danger. It is perfectly fine and encouraged to let the emotion of rage (or any other emotion) be expressed in a safe and private space.

In the case of an abusive or traumatic experience, expressing feelings to a past abuser is not necessary for emotional healing. When working through an abuse situation, please seek professional support, which will empower and accelerate your evolution.

My team is thankful to have cutting-edge systems and resources in place that can guide you step by step to release and heal even what a person might consider hopeless, unhealable or unforgiveable so that you can cruise down the road to your *divine destination*.

Check out the link in *The Invitation To Be Part of Our Community* at the back of the book. We offer acceleration tools for Healing Professionals, Proactive Spiritual Seekers and Light Leaders who intend to share their gifts with others.

Time For Reflection (emotional body)

How are you most comfortable with expressing your emotions? If you do not express them, then what is that costing you? Are you open to starting? Examples of expressing emotions can be taking time to cry, speaking with a trusted friend, therapist or teacher, writing a book, poem, song, etc., dancing, punching a pillow, singing, working out, praying, talking or crying out to God, etc.

_____
_____
_____
_____
_____
_____
_____
_____
_____
_____

No doubt you've heard of or know persons who, while not proven by science, have *died of a broken heart* or passed away within a week or two of their life partners. Do you know anyone whose negative emotions have deleteriously affected their social relationships,

Our Emotional Body

heart, digestion, other organs or caused other dis-eased states over time? What about uncontrolled rage? How might this have been prevented or can it be?

_____
_____
_____
_____
_____
_____
_____
_____
_____
_____
_____

CHAPTER 5

Our Mental Body

"Rather than being your thoughts and emotions, be the awareness behind them." ~ Eckart Tolle

Our **mental body** is the body which encompasses our thoughts, opinions, attitudes, judgments about ourselves and others and the world around us. In short, it is our belief system.

Our mental body plays a key role in our thoughts becoming our reality.

Just like our feelings, our beliefs are fluid. They can and do change over time. The story that we tell ourselves in any given moment can expand us or contract us, control us or free us, limit us or encourage us, judge us or embrace us, propel us or stop our momentum.

In this book, I refer to the **ego** as the fearful, critical voice inside of you, that will prevent you from living your dreams if you let it have its way. The ego's purpose is to keep you safe at any cost even at the expense of crushing your most cherished dreams. It will focus on risks, past failures and outdated programmed indoctrination that seeks to keep you from making important life changes.

How can we recognize when the ego is communicating?

Anytime we think of ourselves as too old, too young, too qualified, too underqualified, too uneducated, too plain, too pretty, too shy, too big, too short, too plain, too broke, etc. to obtain our dreams, then the ego is talking. The ego will focus on "what if" as opposed to looking at possibilities for your life. The ego will criticize, shame, blame, label, awfulize and mock you. It will shrink and *contract* you making you feel as if you are not good enough and always give you very convincing reasons as to why you should not make life changes, take risks or make important choices. The ego will seek people in your life to give it an audience (It loves company!) and agree with it.

Recognize that we all have an ego. Like a scared child, it wants to be heard and reassured. It is obviously not mature enough to run your life, but it is a part of you. When it feels acknowledged, listened to and taken care of, it calms down. Please let it speak and express for as long as it needs to. Then give it a mental hug and tuck it in for a nap or better yet, send it to the beach!

Ego versus Soul

In this book, I refer to **Soul** as our eternal authentic self that is connected to our *divine purpose, divine path* and *divine blueprint*. It operates as our God-Source guidance system. Some people refer to it as their Higher Power, Higher Self, God-Self or I Am Presence. It knows who we are and our potential. It is wise and will always steer us in the direction of our evolution, fulfillment, expansion, joy and heart song even if we go off course. It will bring YOU back to YOU every time. It will not shame or blame. It is the Eternal You, your True Self, and it communicates with YOU all the time through your physical body and auric field.

We know that we are living the path of our Soul when we are experiencing joy, happiness, satisfaction, expansion and contentment in any endeavor. This is not a false sense of joy. We can care for a loved one who is dying and receive tremendous satisfaction amidst the sorrow that we feel.

Our Soul will encourage our dreams and bring to us possibilities for living them through countless invitations and opportunities. Your Soul will never abandon you. When it wants you to know something, it will repeatedly bring to you those experiences, people, gifts and

Our Mental Body

insights to you in a myriad of ways until you "get it." On the road to living your dreams, your Soul will also bring you messages in a variety of ways that you are traveling on your divine path so look out for those confirmations and smile when you get them!

Time For Reflection (mental body)

How do you see yourself? As an optimist or pessimist? What story are you telling yourself about living your dream? What is your belief about how the outside world views you? How much do you care about how others see you? How has your belief system changed over time?

_____
_____
_____
_____
_____
_____
_____

Name a belief about yourself that your family or culture has embraced which you value.

_____
_____
_____
_____
_____
_____

Never Give Up On a Dream

Name a belief that your family or culture has embraced or imposed upon you that you have challenged or do not value for yourself, if applicable.

_____
_____
_____
_____
_____
_____
_____
_____

I often say to my family members that I cannot hear the voice of guidance unless I have absolute quiet. It is true that I receive a great deal of guidance when I am still and silent. It is also true that I receive guided inspiration at the supermarket, theater, beach, through books, music, nature, chance encounters, synchronicities, the clock radio, at Satsang (in the company of those gathered in truth), and billboards, especially when I ask for it!

How do you find inspiration or Divine guidance? Is there a particular place where you are more receptive to receiving it? How much time do you make to listen to your guidance, if any? How does your Soul speak to you? What are the ways your guidance comes through? Visually? Auditorily? Intuitively? Through dreams? Through others? Another way?

_____
_____
_____
_____

Our Mental Body

_____
_____
_____
_____

• • •

Rachel's experience changing the way she thought about how she "should" act:

    A young woman named Rachel found out that the man she was dating was secretly living with another woman. When she confronted him as to why he had not told her, he replied, "You never asked." And, in fact, she never did ask because she assumed that he was being faithful and honest. "How could I be so blind and so stupid?" she berated herself. It was not the first time she had gotten played. However, upon deep self-reflection, she was able to make the connection that her cultural upbringing taught her to put men on a pedestal, be subservient and always be polite. That was how women were supposed to relate to men!

    With that epiphany caused by heartbreak, she began to examine cultural beliefs that did not work for her and made changes. Newly empowered upon the first meeting with a possible suitor, she would ask, "Are you married? Involved with anyone? Do you have any children?" In that way, she would weed out the available from the unavailable men right away. It was difficult for her to ask at first what she considered bold questions but the cost of being hurt and her time wasted was too high. Eventually she got pretty good at navigating dating. She found out that the men she was interested in appreciated her asking questions as well because it gave them an opportunity to talk about themselves.

    Her success was directly related to the beliefs she now held about herself, which were different from the culture in which she was raised. As for the man who used her and betrayed her trust, she regards him as one of her greatest teachers and has nothing but gratitude for the experience they had together.

• • •

William's story: Listening to his ego kept him stuck, until…

A young man named William was reluctant to ask out pretty girls for fear of being rejected. The story he told himself was: "Why should they go out with me when there were so many better looking and athletic guys for them to choose from?" This resulted in years of opportunities lost.

He became sick and tired of being alone and wanted more out of his life. That motivated him to work on himself. He started doing the things that made him happy and went to the gym regularly as well. Then one day he told himself another story. It was, "I am going to ask out a pretty girl that I've been talking to. If she rejects me, then I will ask someone else out. I have nothing to lose because I do not have a girlfriend!"

(After 99 rejections, he finally got a 'yes' and they lived happily ever after!)

• • •

Just like emotions, thoughts are energy which take up space in our body. They can be of a high or low frequency. Learning how to quiet our mind chatter is essential so that we can listen to our God-Given Guidance on the road to living our dreams. Remember true guidance is loving and expansive. False guidance is fearful and contracting. Which one are you listening to? The **Soul** or the **ego**?[3]

---

3   If I had listened to the voice of my ego or the opinions of my friends, family members or colleagues, then I never would have birthed my beautiful twin boys at the age of fifty years of age and lived that dream. As it turned out, I got pretty good at listening to my heart and sending my ego to the beach!!

Our Mental Body

My mental body believes, my emotional body feels, my physical body understands, and my spiritual body knows that The Universe, my God-Source and my guardian angels always have my back. It is a kind and benevolent universe even when things do not go my way. This *loving force* guides, protects, surrounds and directs me (and you!) in every 'now' moment. When we tune into that guidance, the road ahead is so much smoother!

That sounds very spiritual, doesn't it? Of course, it does. Remember our bodies overlap, inform one another and really cannot be separated. Let's segue into our next body, the spiritual body.

CHAPTER 6

Our Spiritual Body

"We are spirits in the material world."
~ Gordon Sumner, AKA Sting

Our spiritual body in this book refers to our **connection** to the Divine or that which we call God or our Higher Power.

This can include our guardian angels, the angelic realm, ascended masters, Mother Mary, Jesus, The Holy Spirit, Beings of Light, Mother Nature, our Star Brothers and Sisters, Mother/Father God, Buddha, Mohammed, White Buffalo Woman or The Supreme Source of Love that sustains us. This knowing, benevolent, omnipotent, eternal force guides and directs our Soul's evolution. It never abandons us and will always point us in the direction of our *Soul's path.*

Personally, I could not imagine living without it!

What are the characteristics of our God-Source?

Your Mother/Father God will never berate, judge, shame, blame, judge, criticize, demean you or encourage you to hurt yourself or others. Its holy attributes are compassion, love, nurturance, wisdom, kindness, mercy, forgiveness, abundance, patience, protection, and truth. Its presence is often calming but it could also knock you to your knees for you to *get the message.*

The Support of Spirituality in Our Lives

Spirituality is a tremendous support in *dealing with* stress by encouraging forgiveness, gratitude, self-empowerment and courage.

When unwell, it can help you get in touch with your *inner strength by* providing the hope and sustenance you'll quite often need to get through with a faster recovery.

When grieving, it will give you the strength to go on.

Through the practice of spirituality, millions have reported *feeling a peace which passes all understanding* in times of troubles. It will guide you in mastering the virtues of patience, kindness, humility, diligence, charity, temperance and fortitude; and that's a very powerful support, especially if your heart is set on living a dream.

Some other benefits of tapping into your spiritual body through **faith** and **trust** include:
- An ability to *sustain* yourself during times of crisis, loneliness, challenge, depression or hardship.
- A greater ability to *accept* and flow with life's many changes, twists, turns, traumas and challenges.
- The strength and ability to *support others* through their dark nights, especially family members and friends.
- The ability to *receive answers* to prayers and *creative solutions* in ways you may not have consciously thought of.
- The ability to live a *more meaningful* life.
- *Greater* physical, emotional and mental well-being.

How does our spiritual body communicate?

Our spiritual body communicates to us in many ways including:
- Through prayers answered
- Through gazing into the eyes of a child or aged mother
- Through a still small voice inside our heart, head or gut
- Through our insights and inner visions
- Through other people or animals (pets)

Our Spiritual Body

- Through physical or emotional sensations
- Through books, dreams and visions
- Through riding your bicycle on a wooded path
- Through organized religion
- Through journaling
- Through Reiki or other energy practice
- Through growing a garden
- Through making love
- Through attending an Alcoholics Anonymous meeting
- Through repetitive experiences that point us in the direction of our *soul's path*
- When taking a bath, receiving a massage, energy work or self-care
- When looking in the mirror, up at the sky or seeing a rainbow
- Through experiencing joy, gratitude or emotional pain

Your Higher Self will guide you and provide many opportunities for you to get the information you need to steer you on the road towards your divine destination. It is communicating with you all the time! So be aware and take time to **look, listen** and **feel!**

Time For Reflection

How do you tap into your Higher Power? What method do you use? How often do you tap into it: Moment to moment, daily, weekly, yearly or just when you are in crisis?

_____
_____
_____
_____

Never Give Up On a Dream

_____
_____
_____
_____

What benefits have you gotten from connecting with your Higher Power? How has connecting to your Higher Power supported you in life? How has it supported you in staying with or achieving your dream?

_____
_____
_____
_____
_____
_____
_____
_____
_____
_____

People who are not connected to or who are cut off from their spiritual nature (their true nature) sadly do not have what I consider essential support in their lives.

In time, not all but many of them have shifts and *find* their God-Source through being with spiritual friends, experiencing difficult times, going through a divorce, experiencing a serious illness, through a near-death experience, recovering from an addiction, giving birth to a child, or just deciding to be open, willing and ready to embrace a Higher Power. And when they do, it is very beautiful because now they can access their spiritual nature and receive greater guidance and support. Please be patient, kind and non-judgmental with these individuals. See their good because actions always speak louder than beliefs or philosophies.

• • •

When you're holding onto a dream
And no one sees what you can be,
There's light at the end of the tunnel.
That light was meant for me!!
So, pull into your heart and up
To your angel of glory
Who always has your back
And sees beyond your story.
There is no-thing that you lack
For you were created in the image of The Divine
Who loves, honors and guides you
Until the end of time.
~ Loria Ra

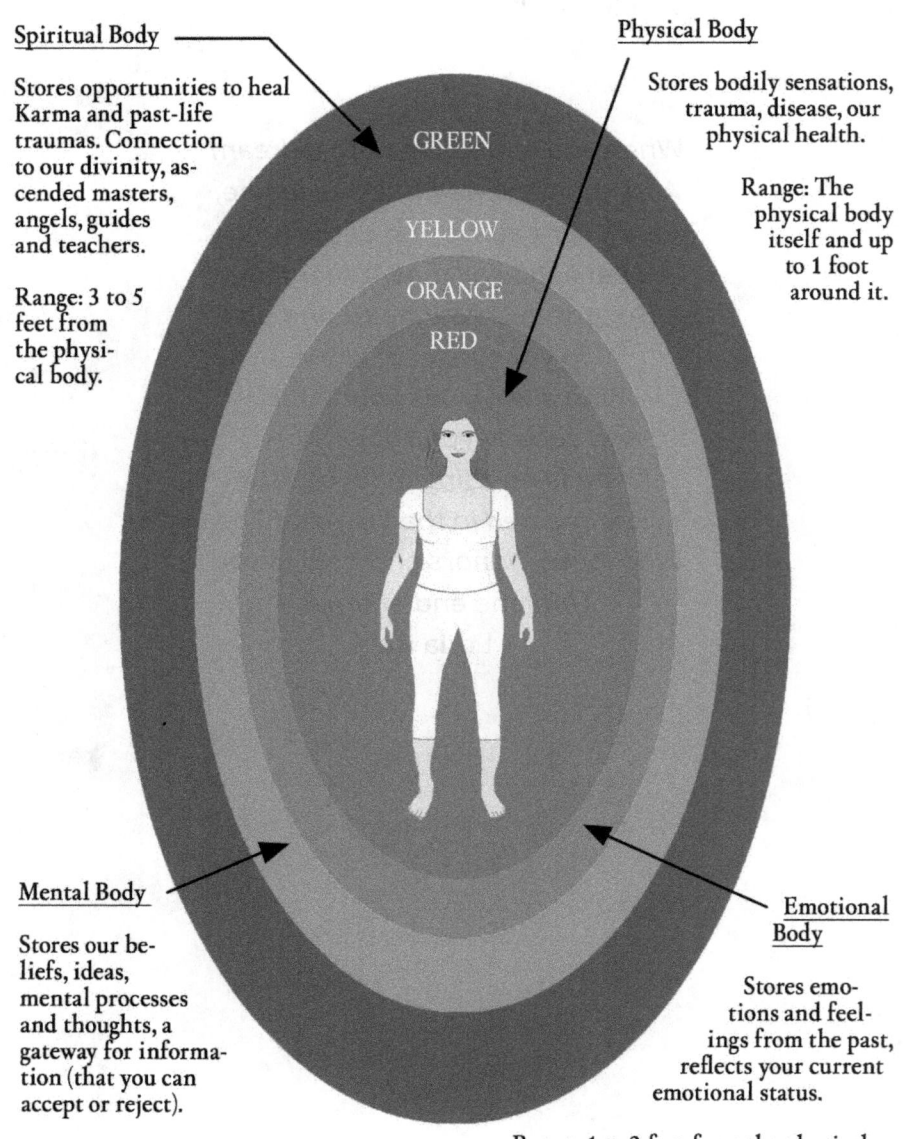

CHAPTER 7

Listening to Your Intuition

"You have the gift of a brilliant internal guardian
that stands ready to warn you of hazards
and guide you through risky situations."
~ *Gavin de Becker*

Have you ever encountered a person who stressed you out by being critical, negative, angry or verbally abusive? Of course, you have. What about an individual who entered your environment that made you feel uncomfortable or gave you the creeps without uttering a word? Something about their ambiance made you feel uneasy.

We can say that we are picking up on their vibrations and, in fact, we are.

Have you ever driven into a neighborhood and felt a sense of peace, hopelessness or fear? Of course, you have. This is sometimes referred to as our sixth sense of intuition and we all have it. Some of us have a more developed sense of it than others. The more we pay attention to our intuitions and insights the more we can successfully navigate the world around us. Our insights convey potent information that serves to guide, direct, surround and protect us on our journeys, if we are aware.

Similarly, have you ever been with a person who made you feel understood and embraced on a deep level almost as soon as you met them? Something about them made you want to be in their company. They accepted you and you felt expanded and safe in their presence. Of course, you have too!

We may say that we are in *resonance* with the vibrations of these individuals.

Have you ever clicked with someone almost immediately as soon as you met them in the workplace, on a creative project, at a class or by chance encounter? You may have felt like you have known them your entire life even though you've just met. These people often turn out to be our *soul buddies* and yes, *soul buddies* vibrate at a similar frequency as we do.

A *soul buddy* relationship is a non-romantic relationship that is mutually supportive and in alignment with both of your *souls' path blueprint*. Soul *buddies* support each other in many ways. They may show up for you for a short period in your life and then leave rather abruptly as dictated by circumstances, or be in your life for five, ten, twenty years or more. Some *soul buddy* relationships last lifetimes.

How can you recognize a soul-buddy relationship?

Soul buddies are not perfect, but they will always be truly happy for you when you get to live your heart's desire. They will encourage you, keep your best interest in mind, work with you, inspire you, tell you the truth and stay loyal. They see your Light, your talent and your gifts and will encourage you to share them with the world.

No person is an island unto themselves. We need each other for support in opening doors to opportunities. We all need encouragement, motivation and inspiration on the road to living our dreams and *soul buddies* do just that. We often call them our best friends.[4]

---

4   *Soul buddies* often travel in *soul groups* or *soul families. Soul groups* incarnate into the same time period for a common goal. For instance, during the Renaissance, which is believed to have begun in the thirteenth century in Italy, there was a rebirth of European cultural, artistic, political, humanistic and economic contributions that

Listening to Your Intuition

Before we get into **The Law of Vibration,** I'd like to continue to warm you up by sharing with you how one of my most cherished *soul buddy's* vibrations impacted the world. She is no longer in body, but her strong legacy is very much alive and well to this day and beyond.

Her name was Sajda Musawwir Ladner, and she was the CEO and artistic director of a community-based arts organization called Universal Temple of The Arts; and she could elevate a room in ten seconds.

Together over the decades, Sajda and I attended a considerable number of events including workshops, classes, concerts, rehearsals, celebrations and events planning sessions. I could not help but observe that whenever she would walk into a room, the room would shift. Everyone would begin to somehow expand into acting more peacefully, more respectful towards one another, more open to problem-solving and become more cooperative. I grew to expect this. She truly brought out the best in people by having high regard for all in the community in which she served as well as high standards for the artists and employees that worked with UTA.

Universal Temple of The Arts is in a low-income, rough part of town. I will never forget the day I walked into the studio and Sajda was having a heart to heart with the hostile neighborhood drunk! They were both laughing and sharing an intimate conversation that ended with hugs!

Those who were down on their luck would often seek her counsel. She always left a box of something free for the community outside of the building. It might have been shoes, boots, children's clothes or games. Everyone knew her goodness and she never ever had a problem in the neighborhood. She was treated like a protected jewel on a

---

(—continued)
took humanity out of the medieval dark ages and into the Light of a new era. Many prolific artists, inventors and musicians were born into Europe during the same time period and shared their gifts including Donatello, Raphael, Michelangelo, Leonardo Da Vinci, Francis Bacon, Galileo, Rene Descartes, Isaac Newton and Johannes Gutenberg to name a few.

block that saw significant crime including homicides. Years into her tenure, she was affectionately named *The Saint of Jersey Street* by a local politician. I always said that she walked with a band of angels around her, and she did!

Sajda had that rare ability to see the *divine potential* in *everyone* she encountered, and people felt that even if she remained silent! I witnessed four decades of youth that walked through the doors at UTA. All were positively affected by her presence, programs and passion. Her influence and inspiration have been felt around the community, country and planet.

Let's break that down. Sajda was only one individual who affected thousands of people who in turn inspired others. How can that be? How does that happen?

It's called **The Law of Vibration** and we are going to get into it in Chapter 8 because it is essential to understand especially when it comes to living your dreams.

Time For Reflection

Can you share an example of how paying attention to your intuition has benefited you? Explain.

_____
_____
_____
_____
_____
_____
_____

Listening to Your Intuition

Can you share an example of how *not* listening to your intuition has cost you? Explain.

_____
_____
_____
_____
_____
_____

I shared with you how my friend and *Soul Sistar Sajda's* frequency influenced and elevated all those around her. Have you ever experienced being in the presence of an individual like this? Explain.

_____
_____
_____
_____
_____
_____

Who in your life has been a *soul buddy* to you? How have you supported each other on your respective journeys?

_____
_____
_____
_____
_____
_____

CHAPTER 8

The Universal Law of Vibration

"We are truly an ocean of motion." ~ Bob Proctor
"Everything in life is vibration." ~ Albert Einstein

Everyone and everything have a *vibration!* What does that mean?
The Law of Vibration states that everything in this world is made up of energy that is vibrating at a specific frequency. Frequency can simply be defined as the rate at which something occurs or is repeated over a particular span of time. You can think of this frequency as *vibrational energy*. We are energy beings!

Everything you see (like your phone, your pets, your friends, the ocean, and everything you don't see, like your thoughts, feelings and emotions) is constantly vibrating at a specific frequency.

Everything has a specific *vibration* and *frequency*. Each note in a musical scale has a different sound vibration as do colors. Each is emitting and receiving energy at a particular frequency. That *vibration* is subject to change. For instance, your favorite beach has a different vibration on a mild sunny day than it does during a storm.

Someone's energy or the energy of a physical space like a forest, mountain range, a neighborhood, a school, or the energy of a group of people is not something you can touch, but it is something you can sense, feel, intuit and react to.

Our *vibration* is something that we can take control over if we have awareness. It must be understood if we are going to be successful in living our dreams. We can shift our thoughts, emotions and actions to be in *vibrational resonance* to that which we want to *attract* into our lives.

The following is how I began to shift into vibrational resonance with what I wanted to create in my life at the time:

> As an example, in my late forties, I made the decision to commit myself to a rigorous protocol of fertility treatments. I finally surrendered! My husband was on board. My doctor was so supportive and encouraging. I was his second oldest patient of all time in his practice to date! Making that decision in and of itself placed me in *vibrational resonance* as to what I wanted to manifest, which was a precious baby. I surrounded myself with women who were successful in birthing a child late in their lives, very, very late!
>
> They gave me hope, focus and a sense of timeless empowerment. Most of these women I did not know personally because I never met anyone who was interested in becoming pregnant in their late forties. Instead of seeking them out, they started to show up in my energy field. (Funny how that works!) I listened to them tell their inspiring stories on television programs, books and magazine interviews. That truly kept my vibration high. Because of them, I became fearless. If they could do it, so could I.
>
> Dedicating myself to my doctor's protocol took my time and energy. I got my rest and took my vitamins. I did everything I could to put my body into a state of receiving a child. I wasn't sure that I would be successful, but I gave it my best shot. Do you see how I became a *vibrational match* for that which I wanted to attract? Little did I know at the time that God would bless me with twins!

Einstein explained it best when he said, **"Everything is energy and that's all there is to it. Match the frequency of the reality you want, and you cannot help but get that reality. It can be no other way. This is philosophy. This is physics."**

The Universal Law of Vibration

Now that we know and understand that everything is energy, and once we match the frequency of reality with what we want (as Einstein said), we can *attract* it. We become a magnet for that which we seek to attract. We become magnetic!

That's it! That's the conscious key to living our dreams!

Make way for the next law.

CHAPTER 9

The Law of Attraction

"You are the most powerful magnet in the universe and this unfathomable magnetic power is emitted through your thoughts." ~ Rhonda Byrne

The **Law of Attraction** states that the things you focus on in your life are what you will attract into your life. What you think, you attract *if* you are in *vibrational resonance* with it.[5]

Know that **The Law of Attraction** is *secondary* to **The Law of Vibration** because vibration is what *causes* attraction. Simply put, vibration leads to attraction.

As previously stated, your feelings and thoughts, which make up your vibration, will attract things to you that are a vibrational match. Like attracts like. Birds of a feather stick together. Misery loves company. If you go to sleep with dogs, you wake up with fleas. (No offense to dogs!) You are what you eat. What goes around comes around. These idiomatic expressions all encompass **The Law of Vibration** and **The Law of Attraction**. Can you think of any others?

---

5   *The Universal Law of Attraction* has gotten plenty of attention since 2006 when the book and documentary, *The Secret*, created by Rhonda Byrne hit the world stage. The book, *The Secret,* and the original documentary have sold more than 30 million copies and have been translated into fifty languages worldwide. *The Secret: Dare to Dream* is a drama film released in 2020 and based on the book, *The Secret*.

Bob Proctor reminds us that: **"Your mind activates brain cells. When those brain cells are activated, you can impact the entire universe! Thought waves are cosmic waves that penetrate all time and space."**

Wowzah! Do you realize what a powerful creator you are?

Let's break it down.

Have you ever thought about a friend and have them call you soon thereafter? Of course, you have. This is called *thought transference*. Either you've thought of them, or they've thought of you and one of you acted on it by calling the other person.

Let's look at prayer.

What is prayer but sincere thought and feeling directed towards our Higher Power. Prayer is literally communicating with God (Great Omnipotent Deity), Jesus, our guardian angels, etc., through our thoughts, emotions and expressions. When we pray for ourselves or another, we direct our thoughts and feelings to that Higher Power and then we wait for an answer. I prayed to be a mother for twelve years before I became pregnant. In Part II, I will reveal the many ways my prayers were answered through the guidance I received from people, events, and my environment.

We Are Powerful Creators of Our Own Reality

Our thoughts are a form of energy which we can direct by setting *intentions*. Setting intentions is simply the act of stating what we intend to accomplish through our actions. Whenever we set an intention, energy comes rushing in to support our directed thought because *energy follows intention* or *energy flows where my intention goes*. With intentions, we declare our intended outcome for how we want to feel through the portal of our heart.

Examples of setting intentions can be:

I intend to spend more time relaxing with my children.
I intend to find my soul mate.

I intend to hike/visit the Grand Canyon one day.
I intend to be more generous.
I intend to eat healthier.
I intend to get my driver's license.
I intend to find my dream job.
I intend to check out adoption agencies.
I intend to find a house that I can afford.
I intend to exercise using weights.
I intend to appreciate myself every day.
I intend to look drop dead gorgeous for the wedding!
I intend to find a publisher for my new book.
I intend to be open to forgiveness.
I intend to visit my grandmother during the holidays.

Goals versus Intentions

Goals and intentions are indeed related; however, different in that goals outline specific actions, have specific outcomes and are measurable. Examples of goals are: "I will lose five pounds within 14 days" or "I will practice guitar for 30 minutes, 5 days per week for 12 weeks."

When you set goals, you agree to adhere to a specific action plan as opposed to an intention, which describes how you want to feel in the moment or the future. For example, "My intention is to be happy with my soulmate" or "My intention is to get into spirituality." Goals involve more of the mental body; intentions involve more of the emotional body. Both are important when it comes to living your dreams and making them happen!

Time For Reflection

What are some things that you have effortlessly and easily attracted into your life? Why do you think this is so?

_____
_____
_____
_____
_____
_____

Intentions work best when they are set from our heart. What is it that you wish to create? How are you going to make time and space for that to manifest in your life? Can you set an intention?

_____
_____
_____
_____
_____
_____

If thoughts and feelings are a form of energy and we are holding on to them, then they are taking up space in our bodies. The feeling of resentment, for example, and the thoughts that go along with that feeling can reside in our body for years creating energetic blocks. So can anger, betrayal, grief, rejection, abandonment, guilt, shame, rage, fear and distrust. If those thoughts and feelings are not expressed and released, they will fester and possibly block us from manifesting and living our dreams. At the very least, they can slow us down. We already discussed how they can manifest in dis-ease over time.

As humans we all have challenges, responsibilities and lessons to learn. Learning how to navigate, use, and release our negative thoughts and emotions are essential life skills on the road to living our dreams. We do not have to stay stuck in our past or our current unhappy, fearful or stressful situation.

Fortunately, there are many healing systems available to humankind today. One such system that I am recommending is called **GPS-Code™**. GPS-Code™ is an evolutionary revolutionary system of personal transformation founded by visionary thought leader, Dr. Tianna Conte. The code teaches us how to shift from *silent suffering* to *Soul Power Sovereignty*. We learn to shift from emotional distress to *soul power success* by running a code. It's a new empowered way of living based on spiritual principles. I enthusiastically encourage you to go to the **Awakening Awareness Academy**, awakeningawareness-academy.com and explore. Remember to click on the Soul Power video. It's a gift that takes you through a daily ritual for soul/body awakening.

Again, please see *The Invitation To Be Part of Our Community* at the back of this book. Through the link provided, you will find Super Soul Power Support and free gifts along the way!

Another very empowering and expanding healing system that I am recommending is called **Integrated Energy Therapy, IET**. This advanced energy therapy system, guided by The Angelic Realm, gets the issues out of your tissues by integrating the pain of the past into the power of the present to bring about the joy of the future. It was developed at the Center of Being, by Stevan J. Thayer, author and channel for Angel Ariel. IET uses the violet angelic ray to work directly with your 12-strand spiritual DNA in safely and gently releasing limiting energy patterns of your past, balancing your life in the present and supporting you to reach for the stars as you evolve into your future. Anyone can experience it and learn how to use angelic energy for personal and planetary healing. You can even send the energy to your pets, plants, relatives who have crossed over, your car's engine, electronic devices, etc., and it will be received.

For more information on Integrated Energy Therapy, go to learn-iet.com and explore.

Both systems once learned and applied have the power to expand us in ways that we would not think possible and set our souls free! Are you ready to accelerate the manifestation of miracles beyond your wildest dreams? Why not take a step?

CHAPTER 10

Affirmations

"We affirm and give thanks, we surrender and let go, we let go and allow The Creator to do perfect work, in us, through us and for us."
~ *Universal Temple of The Arts Affirmation*

What are affirmations?

The word *affirm* means to state that something is true or that something exists. Affirmations are powerful decrees that set forth an ocean of motion towards our desired outcome. They are used for personal and group empowerment, relaxation, healing, raising consciousness and manifestation.

When you affirm yourself by saying "**I AM,**" you are using the most powerful command statement there is! "I AM" is an identifying name of God, the Creator of All! Once you declare those words, you set the creative force into action![6]

Examples of "I AM" affirmations are below. Can you say them out loud?

I AM successful.
I AM powerful.

---

[6] For a more in-depth study of the power of affirmations, please study *St. Germain Series, Volume 9 of The "I AM" Discourses* and the work of Patricia Cota Robles.

I AM getting stronger and stronger every day.
I AM a money magnet.
I AM an unstoppable force of nature.
I AM attracting my perfect _____. (Soulmate, career path, soul-buddy, opportunity)
I AM allowed to say no to others and yes to myself.
I AM loving myself deeply and fully.
I AM an irresistible magnet to my perfect career.
I AM deserving of love and abundance.
I AM in perfect health.
I AM getting better and better every day in every way!
I AM blessed!
I AM receiving and giving in equal measure.
I AM protected and safe.
I AM abundant in health and wealth.
I AM the bringer of joy and peace to all I meet.

For now, know that stating "I AM" is a powerful decree to the Universe and used to bring fulfillment, happiness and peace to all! You can practice using "I AM" with one caveat. Always when decreeing "I AM," be sure to make the statement positive. For example, if you make the statement negative and decree: "I AM worthless" or "I AM stupid," then you begin to set that in motion, and you do not want to do that. Of course, you can correct it with a new positive affirmation. Be kind to yourself always and mind your words!

What you affirm verbally does not have to be yet manifested. You can decree, "I AM in vibrant health," despite being in a dis-eased state. You are calling that state of vibrant health into your physical reality once you decree it.

You can easily find positive affirmations online or purchase books with positive affirmations and recite your favorite ones daily.

Master Jesus decreed some of the most moving and powerful affirmations that you can also read and affirm. "*I AM the open door which no man can shut.*" "*I AM the resurrection and the life; he who*

Affirmations

believes in me, though he die, yet shall he live." "*I AM the way, the truth and the life; no one comes to the Father, but by me.*" These are three of my favorites; as well as this one from Patricia Cota Robles: "*I AM the fulfillment of the incarnation of that which I first drew breath.*" There are many more. Please explore!

Time For Reflection

Affirmations are meant to be said out loud; however, writing your own is a wonderful way to tune in to you. Can you write ten personal affirmations starting with "I AM" and then say them out loud? (Remember every time you say, "I AM," you are affirming "GOD in me IS . . ." When you give it a decree, it is God who is speaking that decree through you.)

_____
_____
_____
_____
_____
_____
_____
_____
_____
_____
_____
_____
_____
_____
_____

CHAPTER 11

The Power of Forgiveness

"Forgive yourself and set yourself free!" ~ Angel Daniel

How can we release our negative thoughts and feelings and move on?

Entire books, programs and systems have been developed to answer that very question. I have recommended two systems that have worked for me (GPS-Code™ and Integrated Energy Therapy™) and passed them on to you as part of my divine purpose, passion and pursuit to share. If, however, I could sum it up in one word that word would be:

Forgiveness

Practicing forgiveness will clear up space in your body for self-love and nurturance. Your load will become lighter, and it will be much easier for you to joyfully live your dreams unencumbered with the heavy baggage that resentment, rage and having to be right require.

Practicing forgiveness takes time. It's a process. Both systems I recommended have powerful forgiveness processes for you to incorporate into your life. I'm going to give you some tips and guide you to where you can go deeper, but first here are some basics:

Forgiveness Facts

Forgiveness starts with you!

Anyone and anything can be forgiven.

Forgiveness is something *we give for ourselves first!*

We are all capable of forgiving.

Forgiving does not mean that what the other person did to you was okay.

Forgiveness does not mean that you must be friends with or even talk to the person who committed a transgression against you.

Forgiveness does not mean that you forget what happened to you. You just don't live there.

Forgiveness will set you free!

Forgiveness, although strongly encouraged in all religious and spiritual traditions, is not something that we should feel forced to do because the Bible or anyone else tells us to. In fact, if you approach it that way, it will not work.

One must be ready, willing and *open* to begin the forgiveness process. The process of forgiveness can take place in a moment, days, weeks, or even years once started. The important thing is to be willing to get the process started.

Are you ready? Are you thinking about getting ready? Not ready but listening? Not ready yet?

What if your belief is: *"I can forgive everyone but her!"* or *"What she, he, it, they, did to me is unforgivable."* Or *"I just cannot forgive _____ for what he did to me (my child, my mother or my family)."* Or *"I can forgive her for that but not for that!"*

Then what?

No worries! I have you covered! Here's where your belief in a Higher Power comes in handy!

You simply state to your God-source with sincere feeling:

"Dear God, no matter how hard I try I am not able to forgive _____. Please do it for me!"

"Dear Jesus, what _____ did to me is unforgivable. I cannot, no matter how I try. Please do it for me."

"Mother Mary please forgive me for not being able to forgive _____. Please do it for me."

In that way, you hand it over to a Higher Power and get the process started. Personally, I hand these tasks over to my guardian angels or The Divine Mother who immediately gets the ball rolling for me. Works like a charm and I immediately feel lighter when I do!

If you get stuck stinkin' thinkin' about how your ex-boyfriend insulted you back in 1998, for example, and as a result, you've been fantasizing about him falling into a deep well for the past two decades, then please recall the following:

When relatives of nine parishioners that were shot dead at Emanuel African Methodist Episcopal Church in Charleston, South Carolina in June of 2015, faced the gunman Dylan Roof in a court hearing shortly after the incident, they met him with words of forgiveness.

"We have no room for hate, so we have to forgive." "God is always greater and because of that, even in horrific conditions, we can still be faithful."

If these amazing human beings can get the forgiveness process *started*, then so can I and so can you!

The Course in Miracles reminds us that "Anything unlike love comes up for healing and there is nothing that cannot be healed." [7]

Forgiveness does not mean we should not express our rage, grief, sorrow, anger or any other feelings we hold. That's fake forgiveness. We need to express, express, express in a safe place. That is integral to our healing.

---

7   There is a wealth of information in the literature that links long-term, unresolved anger to a weakening of the immune system, increased risk of stroke, heart disease, heart attack and other diseased states.

How do we know if we have completely forgiven?

There are several indicators.

In complete forgiveness, we remember what happened, but we lose the energetic connection to it. The event no longer has the power to control us. It feels like no big deal. In true forgiveness, we pray for the individual who transgressed upon us and sincerely wish them well. We do not have to ever see that person again or we could embrace them back into our lives. That's up to us. In complete forgiveness, we forgive ourselves for having attracted the situation into our lives in the first place.

We suspend all judgment of ourselves, and others involved. When we can understand the gift that we received from the experience, we have reached a new level of forgiveness. That's why forgiveness is a process. Please go easy on yourself!

Gandhi said, *"The weak can never forgive. Forgiveness is the attribute of the strong."* [8]

Ho'oponopono

Ho'oponopono is the Hawaiian Forgiveness Prayer of Reconciliation. Reciting it is an easy and powerful soul healing practice. It is used for self-forgiveness over any wrongdoings, judgments or self-contempt and to make peace with someone or something that caused you pain. You can practice saying this prayer to yourself when looking into a mirror as you gaze into your own eyes. You can say each line in any order that you prefer.

I'm sorry.
Please forgive me.
Thank you.
I love you.

---

[8] The *Me Too Movement* allowed women (and men) to disclose their sexual abuse in an unabashed and brave new way. It gave voice to repressed shame as well as spiritual pride for a shared human experience. Why the Movement was and is so powerful was because in order for women to come out of the closet collectively, they had to first forgive themselves for what happened to them. Once they set that in motion, others across the country and the world were able to as well.

Time For Reflection

Forgiveness will not erase the past but will enable us to look upon it with compassion. What is something that you can forgive yourself for right now this hour in full power?

_____
_____
_____
_____
_____
_____
_____

Choose a person whom you are thinking about forgiving. What is the baggage of carrying around the negative emotions of anger, rage, betrayal, etc., costing you? How is it affecting your relationship with yourself, others, your health, time, money and energy?

_____
_____
_____
_____
_____
_____
_____

Can you think of 3 people from your past who you can forgive or start to forgive before bed tonight?

_____
_____
_____
_____
_____
_____
_____

CHAPTER 12

The Love Vibration

"Being deeply loved by someone gives you strength, while loving someone deeply gives you courage." ~ *Lao Tzu*

On the road to living our dreams we are going to want to keep our vibration high, but how do we do it?

We stay with the love vibration.

There are many ways we can stay with the love vibration even if we are struggling. The love vibration is a conscious awareness of the compassion we hold towards ourselves and others. It is the realization that we are all One.

Staying in the love vibration simply means being kind. As in forgiveness we begin with ourselves first. Being kind to yourself could mean saying no to others. Nix the self-judgment, criticism and self-loathing. You are a child of God created in Her image deserving of all good.

Other ways we stay with this vibration include:

Send love to your enemies. Didn't Jesus say something like that? It doesn't mean you have to have them over for tea!

Visualize the amazing future you want to create for yourself, your family and the world.

Limit the amount of time you spend watching the news as the news feeds a frequency of fear.

Never Give Up On a Dream

Spend time in nature which holds a high vibration. Go for a walk to your favorite park, walk on the beach or in the woods on a regular basis.

Make time to consistently exercise and move your body.

Sing, dance, play or listen to your favorite music.

Give thanks often for your life, accomplishments and the grace of God which has been bestowed upon you.

Give yourself a hug, a real hug, then hug your pet, child, partner or probation officer.

Avoid those that gossip, criticize and belittle.

Listen to 528Hz healing frequencies at home and work. [9]

Cook a delicious meal for someone you love. That's you!

Go for a massage, cranial sacral, energy healing or facial treatment.

Make your environment pleasing by decluttering, adding live plants and decorating. Practice feng shui, the Japanese art of placement.

Take an Epsom salt bath.

Use essential oils.

Put rose quartz crystals by your window.

Make love.

Surround yourself with people that truly love and appreciate you. If that means being with just adorable you, that's great!

Did I say be your own best friend?

Stay in touch with your best friends and let them know how much they're appreciated.

---

[9] The frequency of love vibrates high to 528 hertz per second which activates higher consciousness and healing by releasing hormones like oxytocin into our bodies. Oxytocin can induce anti-stress-like effects such as reduction of blood pressure and cortisol levels. It increases pain thresholds, exerts a calming-like effect in the body and stimulates various types of positive social interaction. In addition, it promotes growth and healing. Oxytocin is released in response to activation of sensory nerves during labor, breastfeeding and sexual activity. In addition, oxytocin is released in response to low intensity stimulation of the skin, e.g., in response to touch, stroking, warm temperature, etc.

<u>The Love Vibration</u>

Follow your passion and engage it.

Volunteer your time, energy or resources to someone less fortunate than you.

Make forgiveness a practice.

Smile and eat mangos naked.

Time For Reflection

Can you think of any other ways to stay in and with the love vibration? I am eager to hear!

_____
_____
_____
_____
_____
_____
_____
_____
_____
_____
_____
_____
_____
_____
_____
_____
_____

CHAPTER 13

The Fear Vibration

> "A future experience appearing real,
> fear is something we all can feel.
> Flee, fight, freeze in place;
> either way it's life we gotta face."
> ~ *Loria Ra*

The frequency of fear is a vibration that disrupts consciousness, making us feel threatened and unsafe. It's what makes us disconnected and separated from others. The bigger your dream the more fear can and will show up. We must learn to conquer fear on the road to success. Are you ready to fly fearless?

Fear is known to stand for a Future-Experience-Appearing-Real or a False-Expectation-Appearing-Real. Useful fear can be a warning that cautions us to be careful, like backing up slowly should we encounter a wild animal; however, most of the things we spend energy and time worrying about never happen! That does not mean that we should not take precautions, get the facts or choose wisely. We never want our fears to get in the way of living our dreams. We never want fear to debilitate our progress, clip our wings or stop us from walking through that open door. Fear works hand in hand with your ego to keep you safe in your box at any cost! Change is the enemy of fear but, as we know, the only thing we can really be sure of *is* change, not even taxes!

The Course in Miracles, scribed by Helen Schucman, reminds us that there is only love and that fear is not real. After studying *The Course in Miracles,* I understand that; however, fear does feel very real. It is an emotion that we all must deal with and accept as spiritual beings having a very human experience. We are going to encounter fear and feel fearful at times. We just do not want to live there! Living in constant fear can and does have deleterious effects on our overall health.

Can fear stop a dream dead in its tracks? You bet! Can we overcome our fears? The answer is yes. Fears will arise on the road to living our dreams. So will excitement, passion, fulfillment and freedom to be who you were meant to be! The late great Sai Baba said to his disciples, "Life is a challenge! Are you up for it?" Of course, you are. Never give up on a dream!

Will I be successful? What if I fail? What if I keep failing? What are the risks? What are the benefits? Do the benefits outweigh the risks? Is this worth my time, energy and emotions? No one in my family has ever done this before. I'm afraid that I am not good enough. Who am I to be that great, prosperous, beautiful or talented? There are no guarantees! I'm outta here!

Does any of this sound familiar?

Facing the Frequency of Fear

There are many ways that we can work with the frequency of fear. As a spiritual psychotherapist, I am going to guide you with an exercise that you can implement when you are feeling fearful or even terrified.

I used this exercise every day for weeks and months when I was dealing with a challenging health issue many decades ago. At the time, my fear was debilitating. I could just about go to work and back. This exercise allowed me to be free of fear at least temporarily and supported me in getting to sleep at night. I learned it from the book, *I Come As a Brother: A Remembrance of Illusions* by Bartholomew,

Mary-Margaret Moore, Joy Franklin and Jill Kramer. The book was given to me at the time by a friend who knew that I was suffering. At the very least, this exercise will calm you down. You can use it when you are flooded with fear and it's simple.

Freedom From Fear Exercise

Do this exercise when you are feeling fearful if you can.

Get quiet and sit in a comfortable position.

Close your eyes, place your hands on your heart and take several deep breaths into your heart-space. Inhale and exhale deeply and slowly.

Say to yourself, "Fear is here" and breathe.

Fear is an energy that comes in waves. Observe what fearful thoughts are coming up for you as you breathe in and out and acknowledge those fear thoughts. Do they have a color, sound or image? What are they saying?

Keep breathing, keep your hands on your heart. Stay with the energy of your fear for a few minutes.

Now you are going to shift your thinking. Visualize pink over your heart-space. Recall a person whom you love very much. It could be a family member or friend living or deceased. It could also be your guardian angel, God the Father, Mother Mary, etc. It could also be a place where you feel safe or a nature image like a mountain retreat.

Keep breathing deeply and slowly into your heart holding the energy of that which you love and that which loves you into your heart-space. Keep visualizing pink or as an alternative a pink lotus over your heart.

Soon you will notice that your fear has disappeared. Why is that? It is because love and fear cannot exist together. Where there is love, there can be no fear!

Repeat this exercise as often as you must.

Releasing Fear Mantra

Say this mantra as you breathe consciously and slowly when fear strikes.

Inhale love. Exhale fear. Inhale love. Exhale peace.

Protection Prayer to Archangel Michael

Children and adults alike love this prayer. You can teach it to little ones before bed at night and it brings them great comfort. Say it before your plane, bus or train takes off or while driving in your car. This prayer creates a cosmic cross of protection around you.

Lord Michael before
Lord Michael behind
Lord Michael to the right
Lord Michael to the left
Lord Michael above
Lord Michael below
Lord Michael. Lord Michael wherever I go!
I am his love protecting here. (Say 3x) Repeat.

(As you say: I am his love protecting here, imagine the mighty Archangel Michael and his cherubs surrounding your car, bedroom, deserted walkway, etc. with his energy of protection and safety. As your plane takes off, imagine the mighty Archangel Michael on the wings of your plane.)

Anxiety disorders (of which there are many), including panic disorder, agoraphobia, social anxiety disorder, etc., are all a function of fear. They are some of the most common mental health disorders. Fear can be stored in the cellular memory of our body for decades and

The Fear Vibration

lifetimes. For example, those suffering from PTSD (post-traumatic stress disorder) can relive their fear from the past once triggered. The good news is that anxiety disorders are very treatable. Yoga, meditation, visualization, imagery, guided muscle relaxation and hypnosis are tools used in freedom from fear.

Researchers found out that the brainwave frequency of fear vibrates to a low 4 cycles per second, or 4 hertz as opposed to the frequency of love which vibrates to 528 hertz per second. The emotion of fear alerts our nervous system, which sets our body's fear response in motion. Your blood pressure, heart rate and breathing become more rapid when in a state of fear. Stress hormones like cortisol and adrenaline are released. These hormones are carried in the bloodstream to all parts of your body. Fear hormones are secreted by the adrenal gland, an endocrine gland located on top of your kidneys, which elicits the fight, flight, freeze or fawn response.

Reminder: GPS-Code™ and Integrated Energy Therapy™ are mighty fear slaying systems! Please work with a trained mental health professional if your anxieties and fears are preventing you from living the life you want to lead. Never give up on a dream!

PART TWO

How Big Can You Dream?

Row, row, row your boat
Gently down the stream
Merrily, merrily, merrily, merrily
Life is but a dream.

~ Eliphalet Oram Lyte

CHAPTER 14

Dream Journey

"It is in your moments of decision that your destiny is shaped." ~ Tony Robbins

Along my twelve-year fertility journey, I applied many of the techniques, practices and philosophies that I learned throughout my life to sustain and keep me sane, centered and happy.

The techniques which I share can be applied to *any* dream! Remember most of us have many dreams for ourselves, our loved ones and the world.

When we hold a big dream for ourselves, and in my case, it was birthing a child late in life, we must assess the pros and cons before we come to a decision. Deciding what it is we want to manifest is the hardest part. Once we make a clear decision to go for it, name it, claim it, and tame it, we set the universe in motion.

Be on the lookout for *soul buddies* to come out from unexpected places to lend a helping hand on the journey towards your dream manifestation. Know that as a *Child of The Divine*, the dream you hold for yourself pales in comparison to the dream that your Angelic God-source has in mind for you! Source does not see lack or limitation as humans do. As an example, I did not even consider having more than one child at my age, but through grace, I was blessed with two!

It is important that when you dream, dream BIG, visualize your desire in technicolor with all the bells and whistles imaginable because you never know just what might manifest for you!

Affirm: "I AM manifesting (fill in the blank) _____, or something greater for my highest good and highest healing for the good of all involved."

Coming to terms with birthing a child, getting married, getting divorced, whether to go to university, starting or quitting a new job or career, opening a business and moving to a new city are some of the biggest decisions that we will have to make. These decisions are big because they affect our lives and the lives of others for many years to come.

Most big dreams take time to manifest. How long are you prepared to hold on to your dream before you give it up and get a new one? One year, two, a decade, twenty-five years, fifty, a lifetime, never? I was going to give it until I was fifty-three to get pregnant! If the treatments failed, at least I could say that I gave it my best shot. I'd get a puppy and continue working with children through the arts. I would have a good life no matter what. Despite motherhood being one of my deepest desires, I did not and still do not believe that one needs to have a child to be whole or fulfilled. In fact, I took motherhood very seriously and it was one of the contributing factors to why I had waited so long. I could have well afforded to welcome a child in my thirties, but I did not want to go it alone without a loving partner who was fit to be the father of my children. I have so much respect for single mothers, but it was not the path I wanted for myself or my children. My priorities were well thought out and clear as I began to actively set in motion my predominant dream.

Time For Reflection

What about you? Do you know what your predominant dream is? A predominant dream is a dream that you keep coming back to repeatedly even if you put it down for weeks, months and years. It is a dream that you were meant to have. Predominant dreams are dreams that we are most passionate about living. If you know it, what is it?

___

If you do not know what your predominant dream is, what do you think it might be? If you are not sure, then ask yourself what brings you the most joy or what do you think would bring you the most joy? What is it that you think you would like to do or have even though you have never experienced it? If this is difficult for you, try observing when you feel *spiritually envious*.

Wanting to have, be or experience something that another person has from a stance of admiration, or "I'd like to try that" or "I could see myself doing that down the road." In admiration of another is not jealousy but inspiration. Pay attention to that which you admire, lights your soul on fire or ignites your passion.

___

Never Give Up On a Dream

_____
_____

If you got this far, you are on fire! For this exercise, I am going to ask you to take your dream and magnify it ten times. For instance, if your dream is to own a little shack by the beach, can you visualize it as a mansion overlooking the Caribbean? Sky's the limit! Visualize the details. How much abundance can you handle in your visualization?

_____
_____
_____
_____
_____
_____
_____
_____

Sneak peek: When your visualization matches what you see in the outside world, you are getting closer and closer on the road to making your dream a reality.

CHAPTER 15

Against All Odds

"Never give up on what you really want to do. The person with big dreams is more powerful than one with all the facts." ~ Albert Einstein

I fully decided on my thirty-eighth birthday that I would prepare myself to become a mother. Little did I know then that it would be a twelve-year journey! I told no one! The only problem was I had no mate, but did that stop me from preparing? Heck no!! (I met my husband two years later!)

Shortly after my thirty-eighth birthday, I went to a midwife instead of a gynecologist to get my yearly pap smear and checkup. I remember walking into the office and there were pictures of babies and mommies on the wall. Hundreds of them! I was entranced into an altered state of bliss! I'd come to the right place.

Soon I was called in by office staff who took my vitals, blood pressure, etc.

"So, what brings you here?" they asked matter of fact.

"I want to get pregnant," I said.

"How old are you?"

"Thirty-eight."

"Ever been pregnant before?"

"No."

Never Give Up On a Dream

"Well, you better go home right now and start doing it with your husband two times a day, every day! Run! Hurry up! What are you waiting for?!"

They obviously had never encountered anyone like me.

"I don't have a husband," I confessed.

"Then your boyfriend!" They were trying to help.

"Don't have one of those either," I further offered.

"Are you for real?"

You could see the question in their eyes. They shook their heads and regarded me as some kind of freak. I must say part of me found them quite amusing and the other part was starting to get a little nervous.

In walked the midwife. She presented herself as a lot more professional and proceeded to give me the bad news. "Being you are thirty-eight, your eggs are old and the chances of getting pregnant are slim. Your odds of birthing a child with Down's syndrome is quite high, as well as many risks to the older mother."

She then rattled off many other reasons using statistics as to why getting pregnant at thirty-eight years old was not such a good idea and why in the world did I wait so long? I'm not sure if she would have been interested in my health issues in my twenties, my broken relationships in my thirties, my lifelong dedication to my career and the Arts and the fact that I was not ready to become a mother until then, providing I was in a loving relationship with the person destined to be my baby's daddy who was nowhere to be found!

The guidance and encouragement I had hoped to find at the midwife's office was devoid of any enthusiasm. I did not expect that, and I would not return. On my way out of the office, I once again passed the wall with the hundreds of babies and mommies cuddling and smiling. Despite my bubble being momentarily burst, there was something inside of me that remained undeterred. My Soul knew that one day my photo holding my baby would be on someone's wall, somewhere! Little did I know that there would be two of them! Never give up on a dream!!

Time For Reflection

Given the news that I received at the midwife's office, the average person would probably have thrown in the towel; however, I am not average. I was, in fact, out of my mind. What do you say about a dreamer who is out of her mind and into her heart when it comes to manifestation of a dream?

_____
_____
_____
_____
_____
_____
_____
_____
_____

CHAPTER 16

Find Out What You Are Made Of!

"A winner is a dreamer who never gives up."
~ Nelson Mandela

Everyone that I know who has manifested a *big* dream has ridden the wave of ups, downs, ins, outs, inconveniences, closed doors, disappointments and new opportunities presented, including myself.

We've all said it was worth it in the end but be prepared to have setbacks and time outs along the way. This is where the virtue of patience — true patience comes into play. Combine patience with tenacity and now you have a winning strategy. Combine patience and tenacity with self-care, playfulness and faith and you become a force for what you intend to create; an irresistible magnet for that which you want to attract!

Employing radical self-care supported me during my pregnancy and beyond. Faith and a positive mental attitude sustained my focus and belief that I could do it. Taking time to play during my twelve-year journey kept me sane, grounded and took the edge off. Anxiety and depression are very common in childless couples who want to get pregnant but have not been successful after months and years of failed fertility treatments, time and money.

Along my fertility journey, there were setbacks. Some treatments failed. It was so disappointing! Living in the question and waiting on the will of heaven can challenge our faith which stands for: **F**ace **A**ll **I**n **T**he **H**ighest.

Despite my life plans being on hold, I did not give up. In time, I found an encouraging and supportive doctor who was an expert in his field. He assured me that it was not too late, even though I was his oldest patient at the time! The odds he gave me were a seventy percent success rate once I started a rigorous protocol. I was in!! Pretty good odds but still no guarantee.

Time For Reflection

Can you think of a time that you stuck with something despite having setbacks? Was it worth it? Explain. In retrospect, was there something that you gave up on that you wished you would have further explored? Can you see yourself picking it up again?

_____
_____
_____
_____
_____
_____
_____
_____
_____
_____

CHAPTER 17

What Is Yours Will Come to You

*"If you want to go quickly, go alone.
If you want to go far, go together."
~ African Proverb*

It is essential to lean on your already built-in support team while waiting for your dream to be fulfilled, which is, of course, your God-source connection.

Your God-source connection is enough to sustain, nourish and nurture any dream. It always has your back, knows where you've been, knows where you are, knows where you're going and the path you need to get there. Are you making time to connect?

From there, we build out. Our human support team could have just one other person to start with. We do not always have the kind of support that we would like from our closest friends and family. Not everyone is going to get excited over your dream and that's okay. It's your dream! Know that there are people out there who are as excited about your dream as you are, and they would love to support you. In fact, they are waiting for you to connect with them.

In my case, my family of origin could not encourage, support or understand my dream at the time I was having it. It was not because they did not love me, but because they could not relate to it. I understand that I had traversed waters that no one had swum before in my family.

Both sets of my grandparents were born in Italy and immigrated to the United States in the 1920s. My parents were first generation Italian Americans who maintained traditional values. In that culture, women were expected to be married by the time they were twenty-five or younger.

Women, not men, were expected to be virgins before marriage, despite many breaking the rules! Women were raised to cater to men, look good, be *The Galloping Gourmet* in the kitchen, a sex kitten in bed, do most of the housework and chores, raise the kids, shelf her dreams until the kids moved out and smile about it!

My father insisted that I go to college; however, higher education was generally not encouraged for working class Italian American women at that time. Childbearing was expected to start in a woman's early twenties and end by the time she was about thirty-five. If you were twenty-five and still single, there must be something wrong with you. Once a woman turned thirty years of age and was unmarried, she was stigmatized as a spinster on her way to becoming a dreaded old maid!

Oy vey!

Then in 1958, along came me, a child of the sixties, raised with traditional values strewn across a vibrant background of civil unrest, the sexual revolution, rock n' roll, the drug culture, rebellious styles of dress, women's liberation, The Vietnam War and political change. It was an amazing time to grow up in and I would not have changed a thing.

I emerged as my own person with very untraditional values from my parents. I could, however, make a mean red sauce! When I finally got married at forty-three years old, which is quite late for a woman in any culture, no one even asked me if I was *thinking* about having a family. God and my husband were the only two that knew our plans.

Fast forward six years and you can imagine how shocked my mother was when I told her that I was pregnant at forty-nine years of age. (My father had passed five years prior.) My poor sweet mother started to hyperventilate. It looked as if she might pass out and need resuscitation! She had never known anyone who became pregnant at forty-nine and she was afraid for me. What did I do?

The good news was that after she got over her initial shock, and it took a while, she became a very important member of our support team. As the only living grandparent to our boys, she fulfills a vital and loving role as Nona. It is so great to see how she interacts with her grandsons and how much they adore her. Our mother-daughter relationship has also deepened as a result of me becoming a mother. To this day, at this writing, we are still blessed to have her in our lives.

Time For Reflection

Are your values different from the culture in which you were raised? Which dreams were encouraged growing up? Which were not?

_____
_____
_____
_____
_____
_____
_____
_____

Never Give Up On a Dream

Do you have an inner support circle? What has this support meant to you on the road towards living your dreams? How have you been a support to others in your circle?

_____
_____
_____
_____
_____
_____
_____
_____
_____
_____

CHAPTER 18

Guard and Protect Your Precious Energy

"You teach people how to treat you by deciding what you will and won't accept."
~ Anna Taylor

Building a dream takes a lot of our life force energy. We do not want to leak our precious energy with those individuals who only want to waste our time by feeding off our positive vibration. We call these people *energy vampires* because they drain our life force.

Energy vampires do not really care whether you succeed or fail. They often want your nonstop attention and literally zap your emotional energy leaving you feeling drained and exhausted. They can come off as charismatic or drama kings and queens. We can be related to these individuals or work directly with them. You will feel drained by being in their presence and you will need to set healthy boundaries by limiting or avoiding them completely if possible.

Had I told most of my friends, associates, family and co-workers about my fertility journey in my late forties, I would have received hundreds of unwelcome and unwanted opinions, questions, comments and distractions. Such an energy drain! Most people I knew were not energy vampires. They were well meaning; however, living a peaceful, focused life, centered on my goal was more important than anyone's judgments, projections or questions no matter how well meaning they were.

Being protective of your time is very important because once time is wasted, you can never get it back. Guard and protect your dream by limiting the discussion of it to only those in your inner circle. Your inner circle of support is there to listen, catch you when you fall and encourage you along the way. You know who these trusted individuals are.

Keep the exuberance towards your dream high, as that alone is a force that attracts, but do keep it under wraps with the general public until your dream is well on the way to being born. You will save so much time and energy and be much happier along the way!!

I am rooting for you! Never Give Up on A Dream!!

Time For Reflection

How do you set healthy boundaries for yourself when in the presence of an energy vampire or in general? Do you see yourself as a "people pleaser" at the expense of putting yourself last? What is that costing you on the road to your dream? What would happen if you put yourself first?

_____
_____
_____
_____
_____
_____
_____

CHAPTER 19

Open to Possibilities Is the Way to Go!

"When you say 'no,' you block the flow. When you say 'yes,' you might be blessed!" ~ *Loria Ra*

In my mid-forties, I started to buy into the collective judgment that I was too old to birth a first child through me given my failure to get pregnant on my own, as well as focusing on the risk factors more common with older women.

Oprah did an entire show on *Your Eggs Are Too Old!* about silly women (like me) who waited too long to get pregnant. Being I really wanted to parent a child, both my husband and I were open to adoption and even fostering a child. I was so passionate about motherhood that it did not matter to me if the child came through me or another way. Of course, like any parent, I hoped for a healthy child, but I would have gladly loved any child that either came through me or a precious baby that was available to me. Race or sex were not an issue either. *I was open to possibilities and that proved to be a winning strategy on my journey in manifesting my dreams.*

I knew other women who put the kibosh on their dream by being closed to options. They had so many rules for themselves! Many were opposed to adoption. The baby had to come through them. They did not want *someone else's* baby. There's nothing wrong with not being open to adoption. It is not for everyone, and it is important to *know thyself*; however, all that I am asserting *is* **the more you are open to opportunities the more opportunities you have**. Please file that under: Game Changer for Manifesting Your Dreams!

As it turned out, we did not go the adoption route because due to our ages (I was 45 at the time and my husband was 49), the adoption agency would not consider us for a baby. "So unfair," I thought at the time. They told us that due to our mature ages, the only children we could adopt were eight years old and above. As a mental health counselor who studied child development for a long time, I knew that the first seven years of life are the most critical for molding and nurturing a child. I was not going to miss out on that, so I declined the adoption process.

Another disappointment! I thought for sure we would be able to adopt a baby. Having that door slam in my face forced me to regroup. Back to the drawing board I went. I decided to go back to fertility treatments. This time I would sign on to a rigorous protocol which I had initially not been open to.

Have you heard of this one? *What does a mind and a parachute have in common?*

They both must be open in order to work properly! And therein lies another secret to manifesting your dreams!

Allow me to share another real-life example.

• • •

I used to work with a woman who we will call Sheila Rose. She was a lovely, young, attractive woman, recently divorced when I met her. She had beautiful long blonde thick hair, a wonderful stable career, a bubbly personality and owned her own home, but boy, did she have rules and restrictions for herself! She came from a family of Irish Firemen. Who doesn't love firemen? Her father (who was deceased), her brother and ex-husband, were all Irish Firemen. This is what she grew up with and this is what she was used to. After her divorce, she would only allow herself to date Irish Firemen! No one else. In so doing, Sheila Rose became the poster child for limiting one's options and staying in a nice, safe, warm and cozy box! I believe she is still single twenty years later. I am not saying that it is not okay to have preferences. We all do. We are attracted to what we are attracted to but remember the more you are open to opportunities the more opportunities you have.

Several childless women that I knew around the time I was hoping to become pregnant also wanted to birth a child late in life like me. Once they found out that they would have to get up super early and go to fertility treatments before work, some of them dropped out. Others were deterred by the high cost of treatments. Still others dropped out when they found out that they would have to inject themselves daily with medication to help hold the pregnancy once pregnant.

Cesarean sections were common with older moms. The thought of going through that surgery deterred others. It was too much for them. In my case, I welcomed any treatment that would support a full-term healthy pregnancy. If that meant a little pain, a bank loan or inconvenience, then bring it on was my attitude. [10]

• • •

Time For Reflection

How Open Are You Towards Obtaining Your Dream? How willing are you to move out of your comfort zone just a little to go for your dream? What might you *try* that is new and different on the road to manifesting your heart's desire?

_____

_____

_____

[10] Through my journey, I found out that there were hundreds of thousands of first-time successful pregnancies throughout the world involving women in their forties and even less in their fifties. There are indeed more risks to both mother and baby as a woman age; however, there are also more treatment options should risks arise, although nothing is guaranteed.

Never Give Up On a Dream

_____
_____
_____
_____
_____

Our God-source will always open a window for us when a door slams in our face if we are meant to have our dream. How have you seen this principle play out in your life?

_____
_____
_____
_____
_____

When I finally got pregnant, Karlus had to inject me with medication to hold the pregnancy every day for four weeks. What inconveniences are you willing to put up with in order to obtain your dream? What risks would you be willing to take, if any?

_____
_____
_____
_____
_____

CHAPTER 20

Soul Speak

"What you seek is seeking you!" ~ *Rumi*

During the latter part of my fertility journey, I became more aware that I was being undeniably encouraged by peculiar *synchronicities*. To begin with, it seemed that I was bumping into and meeting women with children and babies wherever I went! Or was I just more aware or both?

The next experience I will share blazes vividly in my mind twenty years later. It occurred when I was visiting my friend Lee in Asbury Park, New Jersey. It was a gloriously beautiful sunny beach day, and we took to walking on the boardwalk. Suddenly, a middle-aged woman appeared, and Lee and the stranger embraced. Lee introduced her to me as Cathy. Next thing I know two children laughing and giggling ran past us in their wet bathing suits, and she abruptly said, "Bye, nice to meet you!" and happily charged after them. Lee said, "She adopted those kids. She's amazing."

For me, what was different about this experience was that this entire experience played out for me in slow, vivid motion like I was in a time warp.

I also recall being awakened out of my sleep early in the morning hours by my clock radio announcing: *"Sixty-two-year-old woman gives birth to triplets in the Amazon Rain Forest."*

"What? You mean there is someone out there crazier than me?" was my first thought. "I have time!" was my second.

Shortly thereafter, I happened to see another *Oprah Show* that featured the famous Australian photographer *Anne Geddes*, who gave birth to her first child at fifty-one years of age and her second child at fifty-three.

"What?! If Annie Geddes could do it, so could I!" It was a done deal. I was going for it!! Interesting is that Annie is a portrait photographer known primarily for her elaborately staged photographs of infants. In the interview, Annie spoke about the joys of becoming a mother in her early fifties and some of the challenges moving forward that a more mature mother might encounter. I must confess Annie was one of my biggest inspirations.

About a year before I became pregnant, I was at a festival honoring Mother Amma, The Hugging Saint, in New York City. From out of nowhere, a stranger came up to me and said," *You are going to become pregnant soon. I feel a male child around you that wants to come through."*

My protective best friend thought this man was being intrusive, but I secretly welcomed his remarks. I also remember an angelic reading I had a decade before I had become pregnant, which clearly stated that even though I thought that I was at the eleventh hour, a child was waiting to come through me; and that there was more than one child available to me.

"*That was interesting.*" I thought and fluffed it off. Before I became pregnant and all through my pregnancy, I kept close to me an amazing book called *Conscious Conception*, written by *Jeannine Parvati Baker* and *Frederick Baker,* which read like it was written just for me! That book provided so much encouragement with real stories of real women who became mothers at different ages and stages. Someone just *happened* to recommend it to me at the time I needed support the most.

In my meditations and prayers, I would connect with the *Soul* of my unborn child before I even became pregnant. We would communicate back and forth. It was profound. All the while my husband Karlus was there for me and supported me and our decision every step of the way. Interestingly, once I became pregnant, the synchronicities related to babies and pregnancy stopped.

Time For Reflection

I observed guidance coming to me from *Source* through the clock radio, books, intuitive readings, chance encounters, television interviews and from the *Soul* of the unborn child communicating with me, which provided encouragement and support throughout my journey. I welcomed and appreciated these experiences. Have you had any similar experiences or synchronicities on the road to manifesting your dreams? If so, explain.

_____
_____
_____
_____
_____

I sent and received love messages from my unborn child that were profoundly beautiful. Have you ever received guidance, messages or information from a Soul who has passed or is waiting to come in? If so, explain.

_____
_____
_____
_____
_____

CHAPTER 21

Act As If, Until the Real Thing Comes Along

"Do your best and let God do the rest!" ~ *Dr. Frank Conte*

Everything we want is already created for us in the continuum. What does that mean? It means that we live in a cause-and-effect universe. The heart and soul energy of my desire to have a child went out into the universe through prayer and a child who was waiting to be birthed heard my call.

In my case, two heard my call and there were probably many more lined up behind them! Those two souls decided that my husband and I would be the perfect parents for them to live the *blueprint of their souls*, learn their life lessons and know God in a deeper way through *choosing us* as parents. In turn, we would be attracting the perfect souls who would expand our hearts and souls to a deeper level of God's love and understanding in the role of parents.

Understanding the spiritual principle embodied in the scriptures *Matthew, Chapter 7:7-8, King James Version* was a source of sustenance on my journey of faith, fearlessness, fire and desire. *"Ask and it will be given to you; seek and you will find; knock and the door will be opened to you. For everyone who asks receives; the one who seeks finds; and to the one who knocks, the door will be opened."*

Never Give Up On a Dream

All I had to do really was remain open to receiving (and boy was I!) and stay in vibrational resonance with what I wanted to attract, which was a baby. In the affirmation below, substitute the word baby for what you want to attract.

Affirmation: I Am open to receiving _____ (examples: a great business partner, an acceptance into a physician assistant's program, meeting the love of my life, a new income stream, healing from a disease, a house that I can afford in my favorite neighborhood, my dream car, etc.) into my life this hour in full power!

One action step I can take in the direction of my heart's desire is:
_____
_____

Remember, taking an action step will keep you in vibrational resonance to that which you want to attract.

If you got this far, you are doing outstanding! I am assuming that you are ready for more. Yes? Yes!

There's a spiritual technique called **Act As If**, which will support you while you wait for your dream to manifest. Before I became pregnant, I **acted as if** I would soon be a mother, even though there was no guarantee. I believed with my heart and soul that I would somehow become a mother, so I began to prepare. I **acted as if** I would soon become pregnant and I became friendly with mothers who had recently given birth and versed myself on all things baby related.

I prepared my body to receive a child. I purchased some baby toys and thought about when I might retire from my job with the New York City Department of Education and take my pension. I even went the extra mile and bought a lovely colonial style house with room enough to raise a family in the school district that I wanted my future unborn child to attend. Was I rolling the dice? You better believe I was but, **acting as if** kept me in the flow and faith of being ready, willing and oh so open to receiving a child, which I knew by hook or crook would come to me some way, somehow. You can also apply, **act as if** in other areas of your life.

For example, while I was waiting to be appointed as a school counselor, I **acted as if** I had the job while I was still working my teaching job. I knew the opportunity would present itself. I was putting out a lot of energy going on interviews and sending out resumes. I knew that energy would be returned to me in its perfect time. I did not, however, know where or when this opportunity would show up. To keep myself sane during the wait, I **acted as if** a new opportunity would be presented at any moment by decluttering my classroom, organizing and setting things up for the new teacher who would ultimately be taking my place. When the opportunity finally presented itself a year later, I was ready to step into my new career with ease, grace and relief.

Apply, **act as if**, when you are waiting for anything to manifest. If it is a lover or partner you are waiting for, **act as if** you are treating yourself the way a lover would treat you by buying yourself flowers on Valentine's Day, ordering in from your favorite restaurant, wearing the clothes that you would like to be seen in, etc. You get the idea. **Act as if**, keeps you in the flow of what you intend to attract. **Act as if** until the real thing comes along just might be what sustains you until it does. You are so worth it! Never Give Up On a Dream!

Time For Reflection

Remember we cannot attract what we are not a vibrational match to. You've heard of famous understudies and sports figures who seemingly became overnight sensations, yes? That all had something in common. What was it? Can you think of any others famous or not.

Never Give Up On a Dream

CHAPTER 22

Stoking The Fires of Desire

*"For your dream to stay alive,
keep the fire burning deep inside!"*
~ Loria Ra

It's important to stay in touch with *part* of your dream even if you are not living your *entire* dream. Why? Because that keeps the fire of desire stoked and your dream alive. It is also what keeps you vibrant and fulfilled on some level. Not having the entire enchilada does not mean you cannot enjoy the appetizers.

When we feed our Soul, we stay in vibrational resonance to that which we seek to experience. The very best way to feed the Soul is through play. When we engage in playing with the people who bring us the most happiness and doing the things that bring us the most joy, we are on the road to living our dreams. In truth, the *creative force* which leads to our unique self-expression is our God-source creating through us. When we are in alignment with it, we feel it through joy, fulfillment and peace. We are powerful and mighty creators. All of us!

I know many people who have regretted giving up many things that they had loved previously, including playing their musical instruments, dancing, swimming, photography, caring for an animal, singing, writing, etc. Many others regret not having started something that they were drawn to and now they *think* it is too late despite still having the time.

Others feel that they do not have what it takes to achieve. Why do some people get so much done and others can't seem to manage their day? What is their secret? It can be as simple as applying daily routines by writing and sticking to a schedule. We can manage time or allow time to manage us.

In the best-selling book, *Atomic Habits,* written by James Clear, the author shares easy and proven ways to build good habits and break bad ones by making tiny changes that yield remarkable results. These little habits and routines performed consistently over time are what he labeled *atomic habits.* '*Slow and steady wins the race*' and '*Little by little I get things done*' are two of my favorite mantras. I have consciously applied atomic habits to many endeavors in my career and personal life with success and fulfillment. So can you! My twelve-year fertility journey alone qualifies me as the poster child for atomic habits!

By staying close to your dream, it will build and build and build. If your dream is to own three two-family houses and you cannot yet afford that, study little by little and learn how to leverage, how to obtain foreclosures, work with partners, save money, etc.

If your dream is to travel the world and you're on a budget, start by visiting nearby states. If your dream is to find a date for Saturday night, put on a mini skirt, stand outside the hardware store and ask, "Do you know where I can find a screw?" You get the idea. Did I say *remember to laugh?*

Time For Reflection

What habits have you formed that have served you well? Did you learn them as a child, in school, on the job, in coaching or were you motivated to incorporate them on your own? Explain.

Stoking the Fires of Desire

_____
_____
_____
_____
_____

What brings you the most joy?

_____
_____
_____
_____
_____

Are you allowing time to prevent you from getting close to your dream? If so, can you arrange your schedule so that you can somehow stay in touch with that which you desire to manifest?

_____
_____
_____
_____
_____
_____
_____

<u>Never Give Up On a Dream</u>

    Do you think that God has not bestowed upon you the gifts and tools that would make your purpose, passion and mission attainable? Do you think that God does not know your deepest longings, desires and that which would make you feel fulfilled? When your dream involves serving humanity, don't you think that God has a hand in bringing to you the people, places, information, circumstances or resources that you will need to fulfill it? Please share your insights.

_____
_____
_____
_____
_____
_____
_____
_____
_____
_____
_____
_____

CHAPTER 23

When a Dream Dies

"The greatest tragedy in life is not death, but a life without a purpose." ~ *Myles Munroe*

It is always very sad when a dream dies, especially if we have held it for a long time and built our life around it. It is to be treated like a death and in fact, it is. We must go through the stages of grieving, which include anger, denial, bargaining, depression and acceptance, so that we can cope and heal.

Healing does not mean that we get over the loss; it means we are free to live, create and love again. It is not abnormal for grieving to last a lifetime. Our great grief is a testament to our great love. When we lose a beloved in our life, our dream of sharing the future together dies.

Losing a child is particularly traumatic. When a parent loses a child, their dreams and hopes for their child also die. That child can never be replaced. Parents and family never really get over it and why should they? Grief is something that they will walk with throughout their life.

Know that when a dream dies, we are at a crossroads. Do we die with our dream? Do we die with our beloved, which means just going through the motions of living, or are we open to living another dream? Although we will never be able to replace loved ones, certain material objects, experiences missed, etc., we still have life.

According to Best-Selling Author and Thought Leader, Dr. Tianna Conte, *"As long as you can fog a mirror you still have purpose."* As eternal spiritual beings having a human experience, grief connects us directly with our humanity. Our breath connects us to our God-given life force.

While we are in our body breathing, the *creative force* works through us if we allow it. That is the gift. When a dream dies, know that you can dream more dreams when you are ready, and opportunities will come your way. The mysteries of life and death remain. Who are we to understand and know the mind of God?

Time for Reflection

Have you or someone you know lost a cherished dream? Have you held a vision or dream for another that has been squashed? How did you cope with the loss? Were you (or the other person) able to find purpose again? What is something that you would be able to share that would support an individual who has lost a dream or a dream for another?

_____
_____
_____
_____
_____
_____
_____
_____
_____
_____

CHAPTER 24

Dream Tripping

"When fishermen cannot go fishing, they repair their nets."
~ Nabil Savio Azadi

What is going on when we wait and wait and wait for our dream to manifest and it does not? We've tried everything we can do to make it happen. We've gotten out of our own way; we continue to have faith and still nothing. We feel so frustrated! We start to compare ourselves to others and observe what seems like everyone else's dreams coming to fruition. We feel defeated and ready to give up.

Have you been there? If so, do not despair. When that happens, it's time for a deeper dive, a deeper look into our thoughts, patterns and soul. Are we giving the universe mixed messages without realizing it? When the universe receives mixed messages like: "I'd really like to get married but being intimate with someone has been too painful in the past, and I am quite comfortable being single, even though I get lonely" or "Arizona looks like a beautiful place to live and work but I am too used to my city to make a change even though I don't like it here anymore," then the Universe has nowhere to go but keep you stuck right where you are.

Most of our self-sabotaging and conflicting thoughts are subconscious and we are not aware of them unless we do some deep inner work. Being stuck and feeling unhappy about being stuck are indicators that there are some paradoxical beliefs, and we need to dive deeper to clear emotional blocks. Emotional blocks can keep us stuck for years, decades or lifetimes. They almost always begin in childhood and if not cleared, they will limit our freedom, happiness and success.

The good news is that we can clear these blocks once we remember where they came from and understand how they are still calling the shots in our lives. I advise working with a trusted mental health professional or with an accelerated spiritual system like *GPS-Code*™, which can take you from the stress of *silent suffering* to *Soul-Power Sovereignty* as opposed to working alone. Please go to *An Invitation to Be Part of Our Community* at the back of the book for further support. There are many techniques there for Soul Power Success and support that will clear blocks and empower you on your journey.

Time For Reflection

Have you ever received mixed messages from someone? What happened? What was the outcome? Have you ever felt stuck? What have you done to resolve this or have you? Have you ever had conflicting beliefs about something? How did that support you in decision making?

_____
_____
_____
_____
_____
_____
_____
_____

CHAPTER 25

Holding Vision

"Dare to visualize a world in which your most treasured dreams have become true."
~ Ralph Marston

    Let's not forget that visualization accelerates dream manifestation. Once we see clearly what we would love to live, then we can embrace it and enact it. Practice visualizing what you desire by making a mental vision board in your mind before bed each night or better yet create a physical vision board. Before I got pregnant, I created a physical vision board with images from magazines chock full of pregnant women, babies and mothers with my picture in the center. I put it on my dresser and looked at it every day for over a year. I was amazed at how every single image on my vision board came to fruition for me — only greater! You can create separate vision boards for career, love life, travel, health, abundance or whatever.

    Visualization is so powerful and goes hand in hand with dream manifestation. Remember, your angels and guides see you as having so much more than you can possibly imagine for yourself. Stay open and dream BIG! [11]

---

[11] There are many systems and books written on visualization manifestation. My all-time favorite is a little book called *Creative Visualization* by **Shakti Gawain** which I fully recommend.

Dream Wheel Exercise

Sit comfortably, get quiet and place your hands on your heart-space. Close your eyes and imagine a wheel about twelve feet in front of you. Visualize the people, places, things, situations and experiences that you would like to draw into your life around the wheel. Send love from your heart to what you visualize in whatever way feels right for you.

Surround your visualization with rose and white light from your heart and sit for a few minutes. Next imagine what you are visualizing is sending love back to you. Now you are ready to spin the wheel into your heart and draw it in. Count one, two, three! Spin the wheel clockwise as it moves into your heart and fully embrace it with hands on your heart.

Sit and breathe with it for a few minutes, then release it and let it go! Practice this exercise as often as you'd like.

Dream Wheel Mantra:
I embrace my visualizations into my heart for my highest good and highest healing and for the highest good and highest healing of all those involved. Amen.

CONCLUSION

Never Say Good-bye!

Here we are at the end of *Never Give Up on A Dream*. We dreamers and seekers know that endings are new beginnings in disguise. To that ending, I sincerely hope that my book and story has somehow motivated, guided, inspired or supported you along your eternal journey towards ever greater happiness, fulfillment and evolution.

My sincere wish for you is that you start to live your dreams. For those seekers who are interested in accelerating their journey with quantum support or who would like to stay in touch, please accept my Invitation to *Be Part of Our Community* on the following page.

Many blessings on the road to living your wildest dreams in technicolor and beyond.

~ **Loria Ra**

An Invitation to Be Part of Our Community

"When opportunity meets passion, miracles happen." ~ Loria Ra

Congratulations on working with me on starting, completing and implementing the exercises in **Never Give Up On A Dream**. It takes time for a diamond to shine but you are well on your way. I truly applaud your self-determination, courage and passion. To that end, I am extending a heartfelt and sincere invitation for you to be part of our amazing and unique community at the **Awakening Awareness Academy**.

With the assistance of great minds and brilliant guidance, the Academy has put together a system of self-empowerment and self-activated solutions for financial, physical, emotional and mental challenges and support like nothing you have ever experienced!

Our mission is to support humanity with *cutting edge products* and *spiritual programs* designed to raise our frequency as we evolve into the next level of living the **Blueprint of our Soul!** However, prior to getting there, humanity (me included) has some work (play) to do!

Through the **Awakening Awareness Academy**, we offer a life-shifting Experience and Retreat in three parts that you can participate in online or in person. Our Academy is one of a kind. It is the culmination of Dr. Tianna Conte's life's work, which she has brought through to support those ready to **live an awakened life free from suffering** with real tools and techniques that are easy to learn but take time to embody called **GPS-Code**™, which stands for **God Source Positioning System**.

Never Give Up On a Dream

GPS-Code™ is a spiritual system for self-leadership that empowers Healing Professionals, Light Leaders and Proactive Spiritual Seekers in their service of others. You can take one part or the entire retreat. I love teaching *The Awakening* part of the retreat and would be honored to have you in my class either online or in person. We offer two person discounts! Go to the link below and explore the many supports our community offers including Holy Fire Reiki, community support calls, guides to empowered living and fearless dying as well as free perks along the way to enhance your bodily vessel!!

Heads up! GPS-Code™ is for advanced spiritual seekers who are **ready to embrace their divine gifts and are done with playing it small!** Simply follow the link below and you will receive a wealth of information and guidance as well as next steps and resources that were formulated to take you on a *quantum* but very practical journey towards your *divine destination* and living the life of your dreams. We also use, educate and endorse non-drug, light patch technology, which renews the body right down to the cellular level. When GPS-Code™ is combined with light patch technology together a *super nova for success* is created! The synergy between using light patch technology for our physical vessel and GPS-Code™ for our emotional and spiritual bodies will truly support you in living your dreams on an accelerated path.

Are you ready to take a step, even if only a baby step? Ready to join the revolution for your evolution? Baby, small, medium or large steps all count! (Remember when we take a step in the direction of our *soul's path,* the universe takes a hundred steps towards us!)

Simply go to: **Loria.shiftandgrowrich.com**

One more reminder. We are *so* much more powerful than we are conditioned to ever believe. All of us! It is so very exciting to witness and participate in systems that accelerate our evolution amidst the chaos of this world. By evolution, I do mean living our unique gifts and

An Invitation to Be Part of Our Community

sharing them, as well as living a fulfilled, happy, healthy, abundant and long life; and passing this wisdom down to the next generations.

Know that our team at the **Awakened Awareness Academy** has **Soul-utions**.

To book a free 15-minute *Exploration Activation* session with me, simply email me at: Lorianow@gmail.com.

I promise that I will listen to your heart and mind with a trained ear. I never pressure anyone.

For now, I wish you copious blessings on the road to living your dreams.

To your love, wisdom and power,
~ **Loria**

About the Author

Loria Raiola-Trapp, M.Ed., spiritual psychotherapist, teacher, drama mamma and angel yogi is thrilled to release her first book, *Never Give Up On A Dream*, through My Book, My Passion Publishing, which was inspired by her twins Jermain and Daniel Trapp, whom she gave birth to at fifty years young.

Loria's self-produced theater credits include *Never Give Up On A Dream, Growing Up On The Rock…The Good, The Bad & The Ugly, A Majikal Musical Winter Solstice Celebration & Celebrate Solstice.*

After a thirty-three-year career with the New York City Department of Education as a school counselor and subsequent private mental health practitioner (she has stories to tell!), she packed it in and settled in sunny Sarasota, Florida. There she resides with her husband and the twins who are now fifteen.

At this time in her life, Loria is focused on supporting others to live a more expanded, joyful life through spiritual programs, books, enlightened entertainment, podcasts and light patch technology.

Never Give Up On A Dream is a guided template for all those who dream big at any age and stage. In it, she provides supportive techniques, tips, practical wisdom, inspirations and motivations for those who are holding on to a dream. All the while she stresses self-care, self-love and fearlessness for the dreamer on the journey to their divine destination. Resources for those on an accelerated spiritual path are included as well.

Loria is excited to announce that the multi-author book she contributed a chapter to, *Success With Source,* went Amazon Best Seller on July 7, 2023. In it, nineteen women from all ages and stages share their personal stories on how they practice vibrational alignment with Source in their businesses and personal lives for empowerment and success.

Please don't forget to accept Loria's invitation
for you to become part of our amazing **Soul Power Community!**

Join us at **Loria.shiftandgrowrich.com**

www.ingramcontent.com/pod-product-compliance
Lightning Source LLC
Chambersburg PA
CBHW060202100426
42744CB00007B/1131